PocheCouleur

Artistic Director
Ahmed-Chaouki Rafif
Assistant
Marie-Pierre Kerbrat
Translation
Linda Moore
Revision
Jonathan Steele Kundra

THE IMPRESSIONIST
Adventure

Jean-Jacques Lévêque

ACR Edition

PocheCouleur

Contents

May 15th, 1863

Frédéric BAZILLE: *Portrait of Auguste Renoir*. Orsay Museum, Paris.
Wealthier than most of his fellow artists, Bazille generously opened the doors of his successive studios (place Fursten-berg, rue de La Condamine) to them. The resulting series of informal portraits of his friends provide precious testi-mony to the extremely fraternal atmos-phere of the beginnings of the Impres-sionist movement.

*T*he date marked the official opening of the *Salon des Refusés* (*"The Exhibition of Rejected Painters"*), created under Napoleon the Third, following complaints about the exclusion of a new generation of artists from the annual state-sponsored exhibitions known as *"Salons."* Rejecting the stylistic models of academic painters such as Ingres, the group of dissident artists identified with painters such as Corot or Courbet. Because of their refusal to conform to its rigid stylistic conventions, they were ostracized by the all-powerful Academy of Fine Arts, an institution which established - and promoted through exposure in the Salon - the dominant aesthetic values of the period.

When compared to the official exhibitions, the *Salon des Refusés* was considered with derision by both critics and the public, who were particularly mocking of Manet's *Déjeuner sur l'herbe (Luncheon on the Grass)*, the most iconoclastic and innovative painting of the exhibition.

Along with Manet, those singled out for the greatest criticism were Renoir, Cézanne, Pissarro, Guillaumin, Monet, Jongkind, Fantin-Latour and Whistler. Progressively, these artists and the critics and writers sympathetic to their manner of

Eugène MANET: *Le Déjeuner sur l'herbe (Luncheon on the Grass)*. Orsay Museum, Paris.
Although it provoked a scandal and the attacks of critics when first exhibited, Manet's painting became a reference for an entire generation of younger artists. In homage, Monet would use the same title for one of his own works.

painting would coalesce into the movement that emerged under the collective name of Impressionism.

They had come from art schools and private studios such as the Académie Suisse (Pissarro, Monet, Cézanne) and the Atelier Gleyre (Sisley, Monet, Renoir and Bazille).

As they became friends, united in a common refusal of the rigid aesthetic principles of the Academy, they would abandon the restricted universe of the studios and paint scenes directly inspired by life in villages like Barbizon, Marlotte and Chailly, and along the banks of the

Seine. They also shared the belief in the superiority of spontaneous impressions over conventional representation, for their vision of existence was as fresh as the new world which was emerging in France in the last quarter of the nineteenth century.

The invention of ready-mixed colors in tubes would also facilitate open-air painting, a practice which up until then had necessitated the artist's transporting a large number of containers in which powdered pigments were mixed to attain the desired colors. The progress of chemistry had also resulted in brilliant and luminous hues whose subtlety and ease-of-use were previously unknown. As Renoir would remark: "These tubes of paint, easily transportable, allow us to represent nature completely. Without them, there would be neither Cézanne, Monet, Sisley, Pissarro, nor what the journalists call Impressionism."

John Singer SARGENT: *Claude Monet Painting on the Edge of the Forest.* Tate Gallery, London.
Impressionist painting was an ongoing and often intimate chronicle of the daily life of its own artists.

Pierre-Auguste RENOIR: *Frédéric Bazille At His Easel.* Orsay Museum, Paris.
Renoir's response to a similar work by Bazille.

Barbizon

Pierre-Auguste RENOIR: *L'Auberge de la mère Anthony (Mother Anthony's Inn)*. National Museum of Stockholm. At Chailly, as at Barbizon (and later in Pont-Aven), painters often portrayed the atmosphere of the nearby traditional country inns. The exchange of ideas among friends over food and wine played an important role in the development of their art.

*I*t was one of the many small farming villages that dotted the nobly-wooded countryside around Fontainbleau. Traditionally an isolated agricultural region, it became increasingly accessible with the development of good roads and efficient railway systems.

The ancient forest, frequented hundreds of years earlier by Louis XV during the royal hunts portrayed by Oudry, had also been a favorite of Saint Louis centuries before. The terrain was varied and rich, with a succession of groves and clearings interspersed with rocky outcroppings. It was an unusual place, whose highly romantic atmosphere was propitious to mystery, legend and love; it had already been a celebrated trysting-place by the time that Alfred de Musset wrote his *Confessions of a Child of the Century*.

Taine would also describe its beauty in the pages of *The Life and Opinions of Thomas Graindorge:* "Under the great trees, one experiences a similar grandeur; they are like calm and happy heroes, and they communicate the same qualities to the onlooker, filling him with the desire to cry out: 'O handsome and powerful oak, reveling in your strength and splendid multitude of leaves. The birch, ash and other delicate trees are like dreaming silent women whose timid and gracious thoughts merge with the whispers

Claude MONET: *Women in a Garden*.
Orsay Museum, Paris.
Women occupied an important place
in Impressionist art and were generally
portrayed with generosity and charm.

and movements of their frail branches. There is a sweet softness in the shadowy hollows, on the beds of pink ferns, in the sinuous paths along the forest floor and on the edges of the small springs whose sparkling waters darken the earth (....) while above, all is peace and light in the inextricable canopy of the great oaks."

Flaubert, in his novel *Education Sentimentale,* evoked the presence of a "painter in a blue smock at work at the foot of an oak, his box of colors on his knees...". His description of the forest overflowed with lyricism: "The diversity of the trees offered a never-ending spectacle. The beech trees with their smooth white bark and their intermingled leafy crowns; the curving branches of the ash trees; then came the thin birch trees bowing in pious rows and the pines as straight as organ pipes, swaying continually and seeming to sing. There were rough and enormous oaks twisting and rising out of the earth, their heavy boughs reaching out to one another, their trunks supporting their powerful torsos, their naked arms gesticulating empty threats like a group of Titans paralyzed by their rage."

In addition to the multitude of potential subjects offered by the forest and its surroundings, there were also inexpensive inns frequented by the bearded artists and their charming models.

Drawn by nature and the unspoiled beauty of the region, Millet and Théodore Rousseau moved to Barbizon in 1847. They were soon followed by an astonishingly diverse group of artists and writers, whose numbers included Caruelle d'Aligny, Barye, Léon Belly, Charles Jacque, Troyon, Diaz de la Peña, Ziem, Ferdinand Chaigneau and Paul Huet.

In addition to the 300 peasants inhabiting the village of Barbizon in 1872, there were approximately one hundred resident artists. The two groups coexisted in harmony, with the former often serving as models for the latter. If the entire population was subjected to the forces of nature and the cycles of the seasons, their manner of experiencing it was radically different, for that which was a cause of sufferance for the peasant-farmers was perceived as mere subject-matter for the artists.

At the vanguard of the rural exodus was Camille Corot, considered a master by the young painters who emulated him. It was he who had first broken the long tradition of studio-painting. Along with Courbet, he had rallied to young Monet's legendary and rebellious departure from the Atelier Gleyre in 1863, followed by the move to Barbizon with Bazille and Renoir.

If Barbizon was the forest and its endless possibilities for providing painters with subjects, it was also the Auberge Ganne, a traditional country inn known for its joyous, convivial atmosphere. The Goncourt brothers, who visited Barbizon prior to writing their novel *Manette Salomon,* humorously described it as a "mixture of café and farm, something between the Cavern of Ali-Baba and the barnyard."

Late nineteenth-century art is filled with images of cafés and riverside cabarets, for although the painters had finally escaped from their studios, they still needed places in which they could meet, exchange ideas and forge a common sense of identity. Impressionism was a collective movement that offered an entire generation of young, dissident artists the opportunity to formulate

common principles, encourage each other during their difficult early years, and construct the foundations for the new directions they would take in painting.

As well-frequented as Barbizon, and located in the immediate vicinity, the village of Chailly was chosen by Monet and Bazille for its proximity to nature in all of its enchanting and virginal purity. It was here that Monet

Claude MONET: *Le Déjeuner sur l'herbe (Luncheon on the Grass)*. Orsay Museum, Paris.
Monet's deliberate reference to Manet's earlier work was a token of the admiration of the artists of his generation towards a master that they would attempt to imitate, equal but never surpass.

would execute his version of *Déjeuner sur l'herbe*, inspired by Manet's work of the same name. The scene was painted in a small clearing near Chailly in which Monet posed his subjects who included his wife Camille and his friend and fellow-painter, Bazille. The sheer size of the enormous canvas intimidated Monet, who never completed it. Despite this, it was an immediate success among the circle of artists that gravitated around Barbizon. A passage from

Ion ANDRESCU: *On the Edge of the Forest*. Muzeul de Arta, Bucharest. Artists from all over Europe were drawn to the forest and surrounding villages of Barbizon. The region became synonymous with a style fueled by the rebellion against the established canons of academic art.

one of Bazille's letters noted that: "Courbet came to see Monet's painting, which he loved. Twenty other painters have come to see it, and all admire it greatly."

Something of its atmosphere can be seen in *Women in the Garden*, painted by Monet in Ville d'Avray. The work also marked the beginning of his sojourns in the villages ringing Paris, whose natural rural atmosphere he so admired, and which provided the backdrops for his portrayals of the "simple daily pleasures" of existence in which his family posed as the models.

In addition to the enormous *Déjeuner sur l'herbe*, Monet painted a series of landscapes which admirably expressed the majestic aspects of nature which had already inspired a number of period authors.

Located a short distance within the forest and surrounded by an ancient beech-grove, the village of Marlotte was where Jules Renard wrote *Carrot Top*. Ludovic Halévy, the sardonic author of the *Cardinal Family*, wryly described the village as follows: "One hundred authentic peasant cottages in the middle of Fontainbleau forest, inhabited by one hundred peasant-families plus Henri Murger, three anonymous bandits and at least eleven thousand dogs.... It's a charming place, and it is in one of these very shacks standing in the middle of the most beautiful forests in the world - in a hole exactly like this - that I would like to spend an entire month."

Like the Auberge Ganne at Barbizon, the Auberge de la Mère Anthony also served as a haven for artists who had escaped the city. Sisley stayed there, as did Renoir, who would represent it in one of his paintings.

Barbizon was the center of an artistic activity rooted in a Romanticism which progressively gave way to the highly personal vision of nature of Impressionism, for it was in the groves and clearings of its forest that the young and innovative painters abandoned forever the time-worn conventions of the Academy for the soul and spirit of nature, of which they would become the visionary prophets. It was a well-spring of inspiration for the movement, whose painters would gradually fan out into villages such as Argenteuil, la Grenouillère, Pontoise and Auvers, whose names are so intimately associated with Impressionism.

Alfred SISLEY: *Cows in the Pasture at Louveciennes.* Private collection. Sisley was naturally drawn to the world of peasants and the tranquillity of country life.

A Concert
in the Tuileries Garden

*T*he Tuileries Palace was the center of all the brilliance of the Empire. It was the scene of fabulous balls, romances and political intrigues.

Although a few of the more bookish spirits such as Prosper Mérimée occasionally took the train to the Château de Compiègne, the Château de Fontainebleau attracted whole groups of merry-makers, for more than any other of the great royal castles, it was intimately connected to some of the most pleasurable moments of the monarchy.

The old protocol and etiquette of the court had long since fallen into disuse, supplanted by the social mores of a new class of aristocrats intent on flaunting their privilege and wealth. Their evenings were dominated by a quest for pleasure and a pronounced taste for the spectacular, played out in an atmosphere which was closer to the operettas of Offenbach than the elegant ceremonies of the past whose measured dignity emphasized the power and majesty of the monarchy.

With the Second Empire, courtesy and respect had degenerated into a thin veneer of often hypocritical politeness; appearance was more important than essence, for one's interior could always be masked by the fashionable superficialities of the moment. The rule was to put oneself forward as much as possible, to see and be seen by the right people in the right places. As the bourgeoisie imitated the upper classes in their conspicuous display of wealth and social position, the wide boulevards of central Paris became the stages on which the pageant of social life was acted out.

The atmosphere of the period is captured in Manet's *La Musique aux Tuileries (A Concert in the Tuileries Garden),* with its undertones of rustling silk, fragrant perfumes and sublimated desire. It expresses the same bitter-sweet vision of society so perfectly evoked in Marcel Proust's epic novel, *In Remembrance of Things Past.*

It was within this brilliant but superficial context that Manet - himself an actor in the ongoing spectacle of Parisian society - would paint *A Concert in the Tuileries Garden,* possibly inspired by

Winterhalter's exquisite but passionless portrait of the Empress among her ladies-in-waiting.

Manet had exhibited his *Portrait de Monsieur et Madame Manet* at the Salon, firing the enthusiasm of his friends and admirers. Among these was Champfleury, the champion of Realism and mutual friend of Courbet, Duranty and above all, Baudelaire. Manet had just finished the portrait of Jeanne Duval, the poet's mistress, whom he called "my old child"; Fénéon would describe the tragedy of her life in verse:

Gaming, love and good food / All boiling within you / You are no longer young, my dear / No longer young, and yet / Your wild life has given you that air / Of things worn out / But still seductive.

Manet's portrait of Jeanne Duval is sensual, vehement and ingenious in its details. It prefigures a stylistic revolution which would project him to the forefront of a new movement. *A Concert in the Tuileries Garden* develops the same principle on an even more ambitious scale in the

Edouard MANET: *A Concert in the Tuileries Garden*. The National Gallery, London.
Baudelaire, a close friend of Manet, admired his thematic similarity to the chroniclers of the social life of the period such as Constantin Guys.

much-appreciated register of the group portrait exemplified by Fantin-Latour.

Manet portrayed many of the friends and acquaintances who had encouraged his audacity and sense of innovation: Albert de Balleroy, with whom he had shared a studio; Théophile Gautier, the brilliant journalist who had enthusiastically praised *Le Guitarrero* at the Salon of 1861; Alexandre Astruc, who had been highly instrumental in Manet's artistic development (a painter and art critic who would later become a sculptor, Astruc was an ambitious and charming man of multiple talents who was among the group of writers who helped prepare the way for Impressionism); Aurélien Scholl, a fashionable socialite known for his biting, cynical wit; Fantin-Latour, who had included Manet in a group portrait which was like a visual

Edouard MANET: *Portrait of Jeanne Duval*. Szépmüvészeti Museum, Budapest.
A portrait of the mistress of his friend Baudelaire. Although the vision is far from flattering, Manet's verve produced a work which transcends a simple likeness of the model.

manifesto announcing a new generation of modern artists; Baron Taylor, a romantic hero who as a director of the Comédie-Française, opened the institution to new authors such as Victor Hugo. The baron had also been an administrator at the Fine Arts school and was the creator of *Voyages pittoresques*, which Nodier often illustrated.

Manet's friendship with Taylor would serve as a bridge between his own younger generation, whose enthusiasm would push him to the pinnacle of his sulfurous glory, and the members of the powerful cultural establishment.

Among the women represented in Manet's painting is Madame Lejosne - at whose literary and artistic gatherings Baudelaire was introduced to Manet - and Madame Offenbach, whose presence signified Manet's implicit homage to the brilliance of her spirit, the product of a century which would soon disintegrate along with the society which had possessed and perverted it so thoroughly.

The presence of Baudelaire - who also appears in Courbet's *The Painter's Studio* and Fantin-Latour's *Homage to Delacroix* - testifies to the poet's important role in the emergence of the new movement and the privileged nature of his relationship to the artists who were forging it.

His enthusiasm for Manet mirrored his admiration for Constantin Guys and Gavarni, who adulated the Goncourt brothers for the same reasons: they portrayed contemporary life in the literal sense of the word, capturing "the elegant spectacle of society and the thousands of lives eddying in the currents of the great city." They expressed the essence of an artistic vision perfectly adapted to modernity, at once the product and reflection of "the perfect spectator and passer-by, the passionate observer, for what an immense pleasure it is to be part of the immense flowing crowds, participating in their infinite and ephemeral movements (...) he who loves universal life enters the crowd as if it were an enormous reservoir of electricity."

And if Baudelaire was only mildly enthusiastic about *A Concert in the Tuileries Garden*, Manet had nevertheless displayed great audacity in his transposition of an historically insignificant scene to the scale of the historic, representing in a monumental panorama a subject which would normally only have occupied a more modest canvas.

Impressionism would ignore the established convention of treating historical subjects in huge panoramas, defying tradition to celebrate scenes of ordinary life on the same scale.

Painting was no longer based on the idealization of subjects placed within mythological or historical contexts, but had become a chronicle of reality in all of its unpredictable richness and spontaneity.

In *A Concert in the Tuileries Garden*, Manet had simply applied to the letter Baudelaire's statement that "No one attempts to heed the winds of tomorrow, and yet the heroism of modern life surrounds us, pressing us onward. The true artist will be he who captures the epic quality of life today, using color and line to make us, in our ties and polished boots, understand the grandeur and poetry of our lives..."

The Family Reunion

Mary CASSATT: *Woman Reading*.
Private Collection.
As in Cézanne's portrait of his father,
Mary Cassatt offers a perfect summary
of bourgeois existence.

*I*n its representation of daily reality, painting opened itself up to subjects other than the imaginary. Even if the models for the Virgin and Child or Diane in her bath were the artist's wife, mistress or neighbor, their personal reality was masked by the overall theme, hidden behind the *persona* of the character being portrayed.

The family unit was at the core of the existence of the French bourgeoisie. The Impressionists painted their wives, parents, children and mistresses, including them in their representations of everyday life and reality. For the painters living in the rural environments of the small villages of the Ile-de-France, their subjects were close at hand: nature, people and the landscapes that were part of their dayly lives. Their paintings were like intimate diaries filled with references to family and friends, rendered in an incomparably fresh and unique manner.

The most representative work of the period, which opened Impressionism to the charms of these very personal visions of reality, was Bazille's *La Réunion de famille (The Family Reunion)*. The scene is an illustration of the family ties that structured the bourgeoisie and which

Marie Bracquemond: *On the Terrace at Sèvres*. Petit Palais Museum, Geneva.
A charming representation of family life.

constituted its strength. It expresses serenity and elegance, a world of well-bred individuals and an atmosphere of natural grace.

Generally speaking, Impressionism would portray this quiet and innocent happiness rather than the more dramatic aspects of daily life in all its horror and ugliness.

Painting thus began to document the lives of the bourgeoisie in great detail, portraying the meals, the women in their gardens, the croquet matches and the afternoons spent at the seashore, as if existence were an eternal summer holiday. If the reality of all of this was somewhere between the acidity of Maupassant's novels and the children's stories of the Countess of Ségur, the cracks that would soon mar the perfection of this vision were limited to the domain of literature, and particularly the works of Zola, Maupassant and Huysmans.

Frédéric BAZILLE: *The Family Reunion.* Orsay Museum, Paris.
In the finest tradition of the group portrait, Bazille expressed the serene atmosphere propitious to the success of such gatherings. The portrayal of a perfect moment in time.

It was as if despite the common knowledge of the pervading corruption of the ruling classes during the Second Empire, the bourgeoisie had decided to maintain the visual consensus of an untroubled existence based upon simple and natural pleasures. The concept of the family was structured by a series of rituals and conventions designed to strengthen its alliances, maintain its network of relationships, and provide an enriched historical dimension - that of memory.

By its innocence and authenticity, the family-centered world of the Impressionists did not prefigure that of Proust's, infinitely crueler and redolent of the cynicism of the Court. Monet's portrait of his wife Camille and Berthe Morisot's paintings of her daughter Julie were infused with an atmosphere of placid happiness and contentment so total that it seemed to

Gustave CAILLEBOTTE: *Country Portraits*. Baron Gérard Museum, Bayeux.
The son of solidly-established family, Caillebotte was the privileged witness of the rituals that structured the existence of the upper-middle classes, including their holidays in the French countryside. The gestures and attitudes here are the same as those in the city, for the bourgeoisie practiced the same mores and customs in both contexts.

have affected the manner of each artist; it was as if the subjects had somehow communicated these qualities into the painting itself. A woman leaning over a cradle becomes the immortal expression of motherly love: there is already a snapshot-like quality to the scene which suggests the advent of photography. In both cases, time is abolished, transformed into an instant of happiness captured for eternity.

Impressionism's main contribution to painting during this period was to have abandoned the artificial stylistic conventions of the Academy for the representation of ordinary reality. In so doing, it definitively abandoned a value-system which posited that art had to be noble, epic, grandiose or solemn.

Silvestro LÉGA: *Under the Pergola.* Pinacoteca di Brera, Milan.
In a sweeping expanse of verdure, Lega's graceful women relax under the shade of an arbor in the warmth of a summer's afternoon.

Max LIEBERMANN: *A Munich Beer Garden*. Bayerische Staatsgemalde-sammlungen, Neue Pinakothek, Munich.
Similar to Manet's café scenes, but transposed to Germany. A portrayal of the pleasures of family trips to the semi-rural outskirts of the major cities of the period, a frequent theme of Impressionist painters.

25

Zola's Portrait

*T*he painters of the Impressionist movement executed many portraits, among them the portraits of other contemporary fellow-artists. They constitute a fascinating gallery of these creators, who often reciprocated by painting the portrait of the artist who had painted theirs.

By its technique, authority and symbols, Manet's portrait of Zola was the product of an art which was not yet that of the Impressionists, even if it rendered homage to one of the first writers to have recognized the movement's qualities.

Like Degas and Cézanne who respectively portrayed Duranty and Gustave Geffroy, artists painted the portraits of their writer friends in natural contexts and among the symbols of their profession. Manet's portrait of Zola was a homage to the writer who had defended him during the period that he was severely criticized by the public and the press. The technique of his portrait still owed much to traditionalism; the colors were dark and understated, and Zola was posed against a background containing the reproduction of one of Manet's own paintings (*Olympia*), Zola's monograph concerning the painter, as well as a subtle reference to Japanese art.

The portrait was the outgrowth of their friendship, which had began in the animated atmosphere of the cafés. Curiously enough, it had been painted in Zola's offices on the rue de Clichy, a few steps from the Café Guerbois, their habitual meeting-place. Their exchange of ideas would facilitate the transition between the academic painting of the past and the new manner of expression to which the younger generation of artists aspired as they progressively united under the banner of Impressionism.

Both in his works and in his vision of existence, Zola participated in a movement of objective realism which found its echo - at least partially - in the paintings of Courbet. That Manet had painted Zola's portrait indicates to what point he was the bridge between two generations. Ultimately, Zola would turn against the movement and even attack childhood friends like Cézanne, while Manet would emerge as the hero of the young generation of painters who saw in him the champion of their struggle.

Edouard MANET: *Portrait of Emile Zola*. Orsay Museum, Paris. Although the work does not correspond to the aesthetic canons of Impressionism, it nevertheless announces the birth of the movement.

The Balcony

*I*t was customary for the Impressionists to represent their friends and family in their paintings. They frequently appeared in scenes illustrating moments taken from their real lives, rather than in conventional poses in an imaginary context. Manet's *Balcony* appears to contradict this principle: the stiff poses are all the more unnatural given the nature of the scene, in which a group of friends contemplates the movements of the street from a balcony.

Manet often played upon the ambiguity of the scenes he represented, while at the same time offering perfectly recognizable likenesses of the people closest to him. Berthe Morisot thus appears seated in the foreground along with Fanny Claus, the future wife of the painter Pierre Prins; in back of them is the tall silhouette of their mutual friend the painter Antoine Guillemet, while his son, Léon Koella-Leenhoff, is half-hidden in the shadows.

The intimate details of the lives of the Impressionists were often documented in their paintings, in which appeared their families, friends and lovers. This can be seen in Manet's pictorial treatment of Berthe Morisot, through the elegant and obviously loving manner in which she is portrayed. Beyond the simple illustration of a gathering of friends, the work also has a deeper significance. For those capable of decoding the image, it offers a glimpse into the private lives of the people appearing in it and reveals the hidden forces influencing their existence.

In their representations of everyday reality, these paintings reflected the nature of the relationships between the artist and the individuals appearing in his paintings. Prior to the Impressionists, artists enlisted their families and neighbors to illustrate historical or religious themes, but none of them revealed to the same degree the intimate truths which now emanated from the scenes painted by the Impressionists.

As in a book, one can follow the history of the young Monet couple,

Edouard MANET: *The Balcony*. Orsay Museum, Paris.
One of Manet's most singular works, evocative of the artist's preoccupation with the world of actors and the theater.

Here, the street itself has become an unseen theater, complete with the spectators on a balcony which is like a private box, contemplating the action taking place below them.

illustrated with the tender and attentive silhouette of his wife Camille in the fields or in their garden. In Manet's works, his elegant friends of both sexes appear, as do the meetings in the cafés, greenhouses and salons.

Degas announced the growing sense of solitude of the end of the century in the paintings of his friends and of young dancers at the Opera which he so often frequented. His portraits of working-girls and women in their baths contained a troubling element of undeclared, encompassed violence and a cruel realism, while at the same moment, Renoir celebrated the ripe bodies and warm sensuality of the young girls who posed without false modesty in the joyous light of his studios.

Pierre-Auguste RENOIR: *Camille Monet and Her Son Jean at Argenteuil.* The National Gallery of Art, Washington, DC.
Monet's studio in the suburbs of Paris was a veritable hub relative to the development of Impressionist art. As a gathering-place for many of the artists of the period, it also inspired intimate paintings of the artist's family.

Hans Olaf HEYERDAHL: *Woman at the Window*. National Gallery, Stockholm.
A brooding yet evocative portrait by a leading member of the Scandinavian Impressionist movement.

Christian KROHG: *Portrait of the Painter Karl Nordstrom at Grez*. National Gallery, Stockholm.
The rural version of Caillebotte's *Man on a Balcony*. The village of Grez-sur-Loing, whose gardens Nordstrom is contemplating from his window, was the Barbizon of northern European artists.

Gustave CAILLEBOTTE: *Man on a Balcony*. Private Collection. Caillebotte's response to Manet's *Balcony*. Here, the perspective is from a dimly-lit interior out onto the bustling Parisian boulevard. Impressionist painting often employed reciprocal references to various points of view, playing off the perspectives between the seer and the seen.

On the Banks of the Seine

*I*mpressionism was born during the development of railway travel and the resulting ease in reaching the countryside. In a certain sense, it could be said that the movement was born on the platforms of the Saint-Lazare railway station.

It was from there that the trains left for the charming banks of the Seine, along which were scattered the villages (such as Suresnes, Bougival, Chatou, Rueil, Argenteuil, Bezons and Croissy) where many of these painters first set up their easels and later installed themselves.

The attraction of the countryside was complemented by the multiplication of pleasure-spots such as the Grenouillère, whose name was derived from "grenouilles" (frogs), Maupassant's condescending expression for the women of easy virtue who frequented it. In *La femme de Paul (Paul's Wife),* Maupassant would describe "The flotillas of skiffs, canoes, gigs, of boats of every form and type (which) glided over the still waters, crossing, approaching each other, veering or stopping and moving on with a pull of the muscles and a stroke of the oar, skimming rapidly onward like long red and yellow fish."

The Goncourt brothers added a more distinctly Impressionist note in their evocation of the "laziness of the canoe floating on the water's current. The slow progression between the river-banks, with the patches of vegetation dappled with shadow, the wooded groves with their grass worn by the steps of the Sunday visitors; the bright-colored boats reflecting on the rippling water, the shimmering patterns created by the docked canoes, the grassy knolls, the freshness of the air under the willows in the grass-filled prairies sloping down to the water's edge and the boat crews waiting out the heavy heat on the grass, lying under the shadows of the tree-branches, their presence revealed only by the edge of a straw hat, the edge of a jacket or a ruffled slip...".

All of this was only an hour by train from the Saint-Lazare station to the island of Croissy on the Seine. The vast pleasure-dome under a large grove of trees included a café with outdoor tables under arches of flowers. The visitors ate, drank, rented boats, swam, and in the evening danced under the light of Japanese lanterns.

To the music of a small orchestra, "dancing couples kicked their legs, the women swayed their hips and revealed their petticoats. Their feet rose above their heads with surprising ease, and they agitated their abdomens and shook their

Claude MONET: *The Saint-Lazare Station*. Fogg Art Museum, Harvard University, Maurice Wertheim Collection, Cambridge (MA).
The point of departure for rail journeys to the countryside and the villages along the Seine, the Saint-Lazare railway station was a subject which lent itself perfectly to the Impressionism of an artist like Monet.

breasts, radiating the heady odor of sweat."

Both Renoir and Monet would immortalize the Grenouillère in their paintings. A few kilometers from there, at Chatou, la Maison Fournaise was a similar establishment that drew a thoroughly democratic crowd of middle-class pleasure-seekers, artists, whores and petty criminals.

Renoir painted *Le Déjeuner des canotiers (The Boaters' Lunch)* at Chatou. It was a typical Impressionist painting, a veritable page from an anthology of the life of this period and of those who lived it. Several athletic-looking individuals in undershirts surround a group of pretty young women whose joyous and provocative expressions leave no

Pierre-Auguste RENOIR: *La Grenouillère*. National Gallery, Stockholm. One of the favorite destinations of Parisians in quest of the pleasures of the nearby countryside. With its portrayal of water, the play of sunlight in the trees, feminine grace and the amusements of the common folk, the painting documents a perfect moment in time even as it unites many of the habitual themes of Impressionist art.

doubt as to the outcome of their encounter. In reality, all of them were friends of the painter: there was Caillebotte (straddling a chair), his faithful friend Paul Lhote (leaning on the fence), Charles Ephrussi, Ellen Andrée (who also posed for Degas), the actress Jeanne Samary, and Aline Charigot, who would one day become his wife.

Pierre-Auguste RENOIR: *Le Déjeuner des canotiers (The Boaters' Luncheon).* Phillips Collection, Washington, DC. The subject was often portrayed by Renoir; here, his treatment is joyously festive, with its delicious undertones of flirtation and feminine coquetry.

Federico ZANDOMENEGHI: *Fishing on the Seine*. Galleria d'Arte Moderna, Florence.

While academic painters still portrayed Venus as a goddess emerging from the sea, Impressionist artists represented her in a casual manner within familiar contexts, as if she were a part of dayly reality.

Pierre-Auguste RENOIR, *Portrait of Madam Charpentier and Her Children.* The Metropolitan Museum of Art, Wolfe Fund, New York.
All of the contentment and self-satisfaction of the bourgeois family is expressed here.

Edmond BÉLIARD: *On the Banks of the Oise.* Municipal Museum of Etampes.
Impressionism captured banal images of life and real landscapes, colored by accents which were the reflections of the artist's own emotions. As here, the expression of the elusive harmonies of a highly personal vision of reality.

Artists and Studios

Pierre-Auguste Renoir: *The Swing*.
Orsay Museum, Paris.
A discreet homage to Fragonard. In his
response to the studied and aristocratic
beauty of the *Escarpolette,* he preferred
the fresh and natural charms of a young
girl from Montmartre.

*T*he villages on the outskirts of
Paris which were incorporated into
the city limits in accordance with the
new municipal legislation of 1860
were charmingly rural areas. Life
there was still provincial and
surrounded by bountiful nature. The
tumult of the capital had not yet
invaded their peaceful streets nor the
courtyards of their buildings filled
with playing children. There were still
secret gardens and mysterious vacant
lots which hosted the games and
adventures of youth which had
conserved all the innocence and
freshness that the environment of the
city so meticulously destroyed.

In addition to offering an infinitely
more agreeable environment, these
villages were much less expensive to
live in than the capital. As road and
rail access to them improved, they
naturally attracted individuals
alienated by the so-called progress of
the cities. In reality, the increasing
mechanization and technological
transformation of late nineteenth-
century society had created a new
urban proletariat which was
dependent upon the city for food,
housing, transportation and work: in
short, for its very survival.

Henri FANTIN-LATOUR: *L'Atelier des Batignolles (The Studio at Batignolles)*. Orsay Museum, Paris.
Fantin-Latour's strikingly dramatic homage to Manet, whom he represented before his easel in the center of a group of admiring onlookers, reveals the elder painter's importance and prestige to an entire generation of young artists.

The buffer areas between the city and the countryside offered subjects of choice for the Impressionist painters. They would ultimately influence the development of painting itself as artists abandoned the city for the nearby villages, attracted by an environment untouched by industrialization and offering an ease in daily living and a multitude of rural pleasures.

If the riverside bistros, cafés and restaurants served as gathering-places for the artists, so did certain studios located on the outskirts of the capital, such as the *Atelier (Studio) des Batignolles* depicted by Fantin-Latour.

The painting was so titled because the artists who are portrayed in it lived in the neighborhood. Manet, who appears in the center, lived on Grande Rue with his wife Suzanne

Edouard MANET: *At Père Lathuille's*. Museum of Fine Arts. Tournai, France. The academic tradition of representing pompously overblown historical subjects was totally abandoned by the Impressionists. Manet, whose palette had progressively lightened through his

contacts with a younger generation of painters which considered him a master, portrayed the details of establishments such as Père Lathuille's, a restaurant in the vicinity of the Café Guerbois, also frequented by the Impressionists.

Leenhoff. Zola was also in the neighborhood, on rue Moncey, and Bazille shared a studio with Renoir at 9 rue La Condamine. Nina de Callias had moved there, leaving rue Chaptal for the rue des Moines, and thereby creating a pole of attraction offering a disorganized but pleasurable mixture of coquetry, art and literature. The Père Lathuille Restaurant (which appears in one of Manet's works) and

the Café Guerbois were located in the same vicinity.

Fantin-Latour executed numerous group portraits of the same type, representing his friends in an entirely different cultural context than that of the preceding period. The transformation was so radical that it was tantamount to a manifesto, and indeed, the *Atelier des Batignolles* was exactly that.

Claude MONET: *Le Parc Monceau*. The Metropolitan Museum of Art, New York.
Despite their natural aspect, the charming public gardens of Paris such as the one portrayed here were in fact subtly-landscaped havens filled with statuary and a highly codified system of cultural references particularly appreciated by the bourgeoisie.

Pierre-Auguste RENOIR: *Monet Painting in His Garden in Argenteuil*. Wadsworth Athenaeum, Anne Parrish Titzell Collection, Hartford (CT).
A page from the period when the Impressionist artists still formed a close-knit community and friends painted one another in the joy of friendship and the energy of a common creativity.

Berthe MORISOT: *Child and Roses*.
Private Collection.
No longer confined to mythological or
historical contexts, the representation of
humanity had become the extension of
daily reality and, as here, often portrayed privileged moments within the
artist's own family circle.

Cafés and Salons

Edgar DEGAS: *The Orchestra of the Paris Opera*. Orsay Museum, Paris. Obeying personal inclinations which had attained the importance of obsessive rituals, Degas haunted the backstage of theaters and the opera, sketching intimate scenes of the lives of their dancers and musicians.

*A*s much as cafés, artists' studios also were gathering-places, but even more selective since they were private and generally frequented by kindred spirits. The conversations were generally about art or literature and often both. They constituted wonderful moments in which the exchange of ideas was intimate and refined, and where the occasional musical accompaniments prefigured another type of gathering at which the Impressionists would become regulars: the salon.

The painting entitled *L'Atelier de l'artiste* represents Bazille's studio on the rue La Condamine, not far from the Café Guerbois. The studio was frequented by Monet, Manet, Sisley and perhaps even Renoir, as well as the friendly observer Zola and Edmond Maire - who would be portrayed by Fantin-Latour - at the piano.

The work would accurately represent the role played by the studio relative to the group of fellow artists who enjoyed working in each other's company and going out on the town together to discuss art, literature and music in an atmosphere of joyous friendship so pleasing to Baudelaire.

The composition of the group was the result of a rapid series of encounters that were facilitated by Bazille's wealth and the endless round of receptions he organized for his acquaintances and friends. He would also briefly share his studio with Renoir (as well as another, located on rue Furstenberg, with Monet).

A spirit of intimacy and fellowship was thus forged among these artists as they circulated from studio to salon in an atmosphere of creativity punctuated by crises, conflicts, and the progressive formation of clans whose widely different temperaments and artistic principles were too pronounced for peaceful cohabitation. There was the circle of Degas, which was opposed to open-air painting; Cézanne's hostility to Manet's dandyism; and Pissarro's modest means compared to the relative wealth of Bazille.

After the painters had sorted out their respective aesthetic principles and were achieving a gradual success with the public, the role of studios as centers for both primary and related artistic activities lost its importance, replaced by regular gatherings among friends in private salons, often accompanied by musical interludes. Suzanne Leenhoff, Manet's wife and formerly his piano teacher, organized

Frédéric BAZILLE: *The Studio on rue La Condamine*. Orsay Museum, Paris.
Discussions, the exchange of opinions on art, politics or literature, and even the informal display of paintings among friends were all carried on in the convivial atmosphere of studios and salons. The boundaries separating each were often thin, and both institutions contributed enormously to the ongoing dynamic of Impressionism (and its subsequent stylistic modifications) in the latter half of the nineteenth century.

Peder Severin KRÖYER: *An Artists' Party at Skagen*. Göteborgs Konstmuseum, Göteborg.
Life outside of the studios was as important to artists as the work they accomplished within them. Here, the festive party atmosphere of a gathering of artists of the Göteborg colony is portrayed in all of its joyous gallantry and fellowship.

informal concerts in her home. The concerts of works by Saint-Saëns, Chabrier or Massenet, which were given in the townhouse of the Halévy family on the rue de Douai or at the residence of the publisher Charpentier, were frequented by the intellectual elite of the period, and inspired numerous paintings by Degas. Mallarmé's salon, rue de Rome, was a model for these cultural melting pots whose ingredients comprised a sampling from all of the fine arts. As meeting-places for ideas and individuals, the salons inherited the function previously fulfilled by the artist's studio.

Gustave CAILLEBOTTE: *Young Man at the Piano*. Private Collection.
Music occupied a privileged place in the lives (and often the works) of the Impressionist painters. References to what at the time was an eminently bourgeois pastime are frequently found in their art.

Paul CÉZANNE: *The Overture of Tannhauser: Young Girl at the Piano*. The Hermitage Museum, Saint-Petersburg.
This simple, intimate vision of the young woman seated at the upright piano is portrayed in Cezanne's inimitable manner.

Turner, or the English Influence

*I*f it was "with a light heart" that France declared war on Prussia, each artist was affected by the event, and each reacted according to his personal convictions. The Impressionist group had already coalesced around a base of commonly-shared ideas and objectives, but the arrival of the Franco-Prussian war forced a postponement of combat against the conservatism of the institutions of the art establishment, the contempt of the public and the prejudices of the juries that selected the artists appearing in the state-sponsored exhibitions.

For the present, all was a question of personal destiny. Degas returned to Paris from the coast of Normandy, Monet remained in Le Havre, Renoir was inducted into the army and Cézanne retreated to l'Estaque. The

war would also claim a victim among the members of the group, nipping in the bud the brilliant future of Bazille, who had so passionately participated in the initial emergence of the Impressionists.

The creation of the Paris Commune would further redistribute the roles. Some artists volunteered or were drafted into the army, others joined the National Guard or other branches of the military. Manet, Bracquemond, Carolus-Duran, Tissot, Puvis de Chavannes and Degas (accompanied by his friend, the collector Henri Rouart) donned the uniforms of soldiers. Courbet agitated for the Commune and was one of the instigators responsible for the razing of the column in the Place de Vendôme. Politically engaged and

Giuseppe DE NITTIS: *Victoria Station*.
Private Collection.
The note of melancholy found in many
of De Nittis' works is present here. The
sweeping, open perspective portrays
a bleak urban environment.

embracing the ideology of the Commune, his revolutionary stance would cost him dearly.

Faced by the gravity of the situation, the artists attempted as best they could to live in harmony with their own convictions. A handful preferred exile: Monet and Pissarro fled Louveciennes for London, whose influence had a great impact on their own work as well as upon the aesthetic of the Impressionist movement as a whole.

London was the discovery of a climate whose distinctive luminosity de-materialized the physical world, dissolving it into soft-edged forms of an exquisite ambiguity.

Above all, London was the discovery of the muted fire of Turner's art. According to Gustave Geffroy, "The talented style of Turner, influenced by Claude Lorrain and Watteau's *Embarquement pour Cythère*, was a revelation for Monet and Pissarro during their stay in

Claude MONET: *Boats on the Thames at London*. Private Collection.
Even more than Paris, London was a city marked by its proximity to the sea. The French Impressionists were seduced by the magic of its special light and atmosphere.

London. They were enchanted by the modernity of his paintings, whose colors were like an eruption of incandescent lava. The atmosphere of thick fog and shifting mists of the Thames had been perfectly captured in his use of color, abrupt sun-bursts and spectral visions of the city. The two visitors stood there in the National Gallery, surrounded by Turner's eighty paintings, overwhelmed by the feeling of a prodigious encounter. The shock of recognition progressively gave way to the joy of discovering that another kindred spirit had already explored and given expression to precisely the same artistic vision that they were seeking. They were filled with new courage and the resolution to advance even farther in this exploration of the possibilities of light. And in the future, they would remain true to this resolution."

Camille PISSARRO: *The Crystal Palace.* Art Institute of Chicago.
The innovative and often daring architecture of the London World's Fair fascinated Pissarro, who in this work attempted to express the burgeoning forces of modernity which were rapidly transforming all levels of society in the latter years of the nineteenth century.

The New Athens

Edgar DEGAS: *Café Singer*. The
Metropolitan Museum of Art,
New York.
Parisian cafés were the theaters and
music halls of the common man.
Here, the attitude of the singer is
marked both by a naive enthusiasm
and a touching pathos.

*I*t all began in the Parisian cafés.
This was the case for the French
Revolution, whose cradles were the
Procope and Regence cafés, hotbeds
of revolutionary ideology fanned by
the presence of Rousseau and
Diderot; it would be the same for
Impressionism.

It was around tables covered with
wine and beer glasses, in an
atmosphere charged with tobacco
smoke, the buzz of heated
conversations and the exchange of
ideas and opinions that the seeds of
Impressionism were progressively
transformed into concrete decisions
and actions.

In the studios, salons and cafés, a
new conception of art was being
forged. All that remained was to
find walls on which to exhibit it.

The road to success would be
long. From 1863 (the year of the
Salon des Refusés) to 1874 (the First
Impressionist Exhibition at Nadar's
studio), it would take ten years of
struggle for their talent to be
revealed to the world.

In the genealogy of the cafés
linked to the emergence of
Impressionism, the precursor was the
Brasserie des Martyrs, frequented by
Courbet, who held forth among a
group of young admirers which

Edgar DEGAS: *The Absinthe Drinker.*
Orsay Museum, Paris.
As gathering places for all levels of
society, cafés were also the stages on
which human dramas were played out
before an indifferent public. Ellen
Andrée, a minor actress, and Marcelin
Desboutins, a vague acquaintance of
Degas, posed for this striking scene in
which one can easily imagine Verlaine
or Rimbaud participating as the
supporting cast.

Jean-Louis FORAIN: *At the Nouvelle-Athènes*. Louvre Museum, Paris.
Along with the nearby Guerbois, this celebrated artists' café on Place Pigalle was one of the habitual gathering places of the Impressionist painters. The scene is a typical vision of the artistic life of the period.

included Baudelaire, Champfleury, Castagnary, Théodore de Banville and the ubiquitous Doctor Gachet.

Even more intimately linked to the early years of Impressionism was the Café Guerbois, named after its founder and located at 11 Grande-Rue des Batignolles. There was the corner reserved for artists, "two tables to the left of the door" where Manet - who was the central figure and already in the public's eye - was joined by Fantin-Latour, Stevens, Whistler,

migrate to the Nouvelle-Athènes, a café on Place Pigalle, close to the studios of Degas and Renoir.

The writer George Moore, who was a regular, spoke of "the glass door scraping the sand sprinkled on the floor" when clients entered. He evoked the "odors of each hour: in the morning, the smell of eggs frying in butter and the sharp scent of cigarette smoke and bad cognac; at five, the plant-like perfume of Absinthe; shortly after, the vapor of

Alexandre Astruc, De Nittis, Degas, Marcellin, Desboutin, Bazille, Renoir, Guillaumin, Bracquemond, Nadar, Guigou, Sisley, Monet, Pissarro, Zola, and Paul Alexis as well as Cézanne when he was in Paris.

As Manet would confess in the atmosphere of war in 1870, before the Franco-Prussian conflict would scatter the artists who gathered there, "The Café Guerbois is my unique haven." Many of these same artists would

Edgar DEGAS: *Women on a Café Terrace*. Orsay Museum, Paris. Degas emphasizes the effect of the artificial lighting, in which the women occupy a multiple and ambiguous dimension, the reflection of their social status during this period.

hot soup and as the evening advances, cigarettes, café and beer. A low partition, just a few inches higher that the heads of the clients, divides the main room and its marble tables...". Suzanne Valadon, who at that time was still an artists' model, was painted by Zandomeneghi in the reflection of the luminous globes and tall wall-mirrors which decorated the café. It was similar to the vision of the café as seen by Caillebotte, with its multiple of reflections and perspectives.

As a space of exchange and communication, an amplifier of public opinion, the café was one of the essential elements of artistic life as well as a favorite subject for the painters who had totally adopted it as part of their daily existence.

Each artist represented the cafés according to his own temperament. Manet portrayed a festive atmosphere marked by an attitude of complicity toward the frank sensuality of the women who populated his scenes, in

Gustave CAILLEBOTTE: *The Card Game.* Private Collection.
Another aspect of life in the Parisian cafés (here, the interior is distinctly bourgeois): endless card games among friends. The sober and exclusively masculine atmosphere precludes any suggestion of the opposite sex.

which the mixture of flirtation and coquetry reflected the fantasies of the bourgeoisie. Degas chose a more dramatic vision, focusing on the dimension of solitude that was present beneath their convivial surface, and which can be seen in the

bitter pathos of *L'Absinthe (The Absinthe Drinker)*. For all of its pleasures, the café could also be the setting for all of existence's solitary pain: Verlaine himself could have posed for Degas' intensely personal vision.

Gustave CAILLEBOTTE: *At the Café*. Museum of Fine Arts. Rouen, France. The habitual café-goer possessed his or her own distinctive manner of appearing on the stage of these strange theaters which inspired many the characters appearing in the plays of the dramatist Courteline.

The Studio
on Rue Saint-Georges

*A*fter ascending with
determination the flanks of lower
Montmartre, the rue Saint-Georges
collides against the agitated shoals of
a wide boulevard that intersects it
perpendicularly. Degas was born at
number 8; although his family was
distinctly bourgeois, their
neighborhood was a disparate
patchwork of social classes, on whose
fringes lived the characters described
by Henry Murger in his *Scènes de la
vie de Bohème.* The joyously non-
conformist atmosphere of the
neighborhood would impregnate the
lives and works of the young
painters with its air of innocent
frivolity and distinctly populist
orientation.

Like many of his fellow-artists,
Renoir, whose reputation as a
painter was already growing,
nevertheless suffered from the
rigidity of the Jury of the Salon,
which had rejected two of his
favorite works: *La Rose* and *Cavaliers
au bois de Boulogne (Riders
in the Bois de Boulogne).*

His encounter with Théodore
Duret, an art-lover and erstwhile art
merchant who had purchased several
of his paintings, gave him the
opportunity of taking a studio at 35
rue Saint-Georges, near the Café
Guerbois, the gathering-place of his
friends. The address would become
part of the history of Impressionism.

The neighborhood was also
home to many of the academic
painters who practiced their art in an
atmosphere of luxury and
ostentation. Their studio-residences,
with their medieval decor and subtle
oriental touches, were frequented by
aristocrats and the elite. Here,
between candelabras and soft
cushions, suits of armor and
curtained alcoves, they contemplated
the overblown paintings of scantily-
clad nymphs and goddesses which
so charmed the women even as they
titillated their male companions.

Renoir's studio was soberly
appointed with well-worn furniture,
brightened here and there by a
negligently-thrown bolt of colored
fabric. His models were often nude or
represented lightly draped; refusing
the conventional poses of the Venuses
of the period, he invented sensual
odalisques.

Among his neighbors were the
Goncourt brothers, who chronicled
social and intellectual life from their
palatial residence filled with art
objects, oriental bric-a-brac, and the
young women of easy virtue who
were one of the features of the area in
which they lived.

The frank sensuality of the

Gustave CAILLEBOTTE: *Place Saint-Georges*. Private Collection.
In late nineteenth-century Paris, Place Saint-Georges was a cross-roads of artistic life located between the wide new boulevards of the center city and the semi-rural charms of Montmartre, situated just above it.

Claude MONET: *The Luncheon*. Orsay Museum, Paris.

The scene contains all of the elements common to a movement in total opposition to the academic canons of art that still dominated the period. Refusing any reference to history or mythology, it captured ordinary yet often charming everyday scenes of the immediate environment or intimate moments of family life. As here, the artist's vision was generally of the simple pleasures of existence.

neighborhood would impregnate Renoir's work as he exchanged ideas and projects with Monet, whom he often visited on sun-filled afternoons in the gardens of his home in Argenteuil.

The studio on the rue Saint-Georges was not only a place for painting; the gatherings often held there were the continuation of those begun at the nearby Café Guerbois and Nouvelle-Athènes. It was in Monet's studio that the group founded *La Société anonyme coopérative des artistes peintres, sculpteurs et graveurs (The Co-operative Association of Painters, Sculptors and Engravers)* which

organized the First Impressionist Exhibition.

A charter for the organization was signed by de Molins, Renoir, Cals, Rouart, Monet, Degas, Latouche, Bur472eau, Sisley, Robert, the Ottins, Colin and Béliard, all of whom would hang their works at Nadar's studio, where the first exhibition was held.

Pierre-Auguste RENOIR: *Riders in the Bois de Boulogne*. Hamburger Kunsthalle, Hamburg.
Like Manet's *A Concert in the Tuileries Garden*, Renoir portrayed members of the Parisian bourgeoisie in a moment of leisure typical of their class.

The Triumph of Impressionism

First Exhibition, 1874

*I*mpression, soleil levant
(Impression, Rising Sun) was painted
in 1872. Monet had returned from
England and was passing his time
between the Hôtel de Londres et de
New York in front of the Saint-Lazare
station, his studio at 8 rue d'Isly and
the suburban village of Argenteuil,
where Manet had found him a house
surrounded by an enormous garden
near the banks of the Seine. Perhaps
a sign of destiny, it had previously
been occupied by Théodule Ribot and
briefly by Renoir.

This bucolic setting progressively
became a gathering-place for Monet's
friends from Paris. He would
subsequently move to another house
in the same village, this time facing
the railway station at 2 boulevard
Saint-Denis.

The period marked the
emergence of the themes of gardens,
rivers, boating, and women and
children surrounded by nature whose
similarity was a principal characteristic
of the Impressionists. Despite his
financial difficulties, the art dealer
Durand-Ruel, who had up until then
been interested by the naturalists of

the Barbizon School, began to buy
works by Pissarro, Degas, Sisley,
Renoir and Monet.

These were years of a rich and
intense activity, in which artists began
to open their styles to express
feelings, sensations and the instability
of material forms, painting subjects
with a new and heady sense of
liberty.

Both Sisley and Renoir were
caught up by the energy of the
movement; Manet portrayed his
friend Monet aboard the boat-studio
moored on the Seine, similar to that
of Daubigny, who had his own on
the Oise at Auvers.

The hostility of the Salon toward
this small group of like-minded
painters confirmed their belief that the
only way to show their works was by
organizing their own exhibition. After
continuing the discussions which had
begun in Renoir's studio on the rue
Saint-Georges, it was decided to hold
the exhibition in Nadar's studio in
April 1874. The date marked the
beginning of the official existence of
the Impressionists and of their integration into the cultural life of the period.

Claude MONET: *Impression, Rising
Sun.* Marmottan Museum, Paris.
This unassuming, spontaneous and
essentially modest painting would
become the emblem of the Impressionist movement. Monet's work prefigures
all of his later stylistic innovations.

Curiously, the name "Impressionist" was coined during a visit to the exhibition by a journalist hostile to the movement:

- "I don't understand the subject of this painting. What's the title?

- *Impression, Rising Sun.*

- I thought so: since I'm so impressed, there must be some impressions in it. And what liberty, what freedom of technique! A roll of wall-paper is more artistic than this painting."

Once it had been created, the expression became part of the general vocabulary. Gustave Geffroy, the first art historian to study Monet's works, also attributed its origin to Monet: "It was Monet who unwittingly created the expression by using the word *'Impression'* in the title of one of his paintings."

Paul CÉZANNE: *The House of the Hanged-Man.* Orsay Museum, Paris. From the very beginning of his career as a painter, Cézanne's manner was different from that of his fellow artists. His scenes were carefully constructed, geometrical compositions expressing everyday reality. Pissarro would have a determining influence on his progress as an artist, freeing him from the internal contradictions which had previously inhibited his stylistic development, and opening the way to a totally new form of painting.

As the unofficial leader of the movement, Monet was the center of a galaxy of lesser-known artists such as Attendu, Béliard, Brandon, Bureau, Cals, Debras, Latouche, Levert, Meyer, de Molins, Mulot-Durivage, Ottin (Auguste and Léon) and Léon-Paul Robert. Still others would associate themselves with the group: Astruc, whose energy and enthusiasm so impressed his fellow-painters; Félix Bracquemond, the talented engraver; Boudin, their spiritual god-father; Guillaumin, who would soon emerge from the obscurity of crushing poverty; Lepic, a close friend of Degas and known for his mastery of technique; de Nittis, active on all fronts, including the official Salon; Henri Rouart, a well-known collector and amateur painter whose works were of a

Camille PISSARRO: *Chestnut Trees at Osny*. Private Collection.
The representation of nature by the Impressionist painters was the logical extension of an earlier manner known as Naturalism. In many of his works, Pissarro would endow nature with a supplementary dimension of subtle social commentary.

Berthe MORISOT: *The Cradle*. Orsay
Museum, Paris.
One of the major aspects of Impressionist art was its portrayal of intimate
scenes of family life. Here, the painter
Berthe Morisot offers a touching vision
of her own experience as a young
mother.

quality sufficient to warrant his inclusion in the group.

There were also the authentically great artists and those who would become so: Sisley, Renoir, Pissarro, Morisot, Degas and Cézanne. Even if only a few of their works were on view, they were already among the movement's most representative examples: *La Maison du pendu (The House of the Hanged-Man)* by Cézanne, *Intérieur de coulisse (Backstage interior)* and *La Blanchisseuse (The Washerwoman)* by Degas, *Le Berceau (The Cradle)* by Berthe Morisot, Renoir's *La Loge (The Theater Box)*, Sisley's *La Seine à Port-Marly (The Seine at Port-Marly)* and Pissarro's *Les Châtaigniers d'Osny (Chestnut Trees at Osny)* incarnated the stylistic elements associated with Impressionism.

Edgar DEGAS: *Horse Races in the Provinces*. Museum of Fine Arts, Boston (MA).
Fascinated by the physical aspect and graceful movement of horses, Degas frequently attended horse races and portrayed their less-obvious social aspects in paintings such as this.

The Disastrous Sale of 1875

The following year (1875) was catastrophic for the movement. Unable to surmount the hostility of public opinion and the press, the group began to disintegrate. The works of Monet, Berthe Morisot, Renoir and Sisley were auctioned off at rock-bottom prices.

The preface of the auction catalogue was written by Philippe Burty, a close friend of the Goncourt brothers; in the auction-house, the public's anger was so great that the police were called in to prevent their protests from turning into a full-scale riot.

In financial terms, the sale was disastrous: 300 francs for Monet's *Etude de neige (Snow)* and even less for his *Coucher de soleil sur la Seine (Sunset on the Seine)* and *La Neige à Argenteuil (Snow at Argenteuil)*; 100

Pierre-Auguste RENOIR: *Pont Neuf*. The National Gallery of Art, Washington, DC.
Even more than the architectural elements, Renoir was interested in capturing the ephemeral, human aspects of the city.

and 130 francs for Sisley's *Bougival* and *Temps de neige (Snowy Weather)*; 220 and 300 francs for Renoir's *Avant-scène (The Stage)* and *Pont-Neuf*; 210 and 320 francs for Berthe Morisot's *La Lecture (Reading)* and *Sur l'herbe (On the Grass)*.

Victor Chocquet found himself intimately involved with the Impressionists. After having Renoir paint his portrait, he encountered Cézanne, and one of the most astonishing adventures in the history of modern art collections began.

Berthe MORISOT: *Reading*. The National Gallery of Art, Chester Dale Collection, Washington, DC. Like Fantin-Latour, Morisot often portrayed intimate aspects of family life among the bourgeoisie.

71

Second Exhibition, 1876

"An unfortunate event has occurred on rue Le Peletier. After the fire at the Opera, a new disaster has hit the neighborhood: it is an exhibition by so-called painters. The innocent passer-by, attracted by the flags decorating the front of the gallery, enters and is confronted by a horrible sight: five or six mentally deranged individuals - of which one is a woman - and all suffering from an excess of ambition, have gathered here to exhibit their works. Some people would only laugh at such pretentiousness. As for myself, I was sickened. These so-called artists are known as Impressionists; they take a canvas, paint and brushes, throw them all together in any way they can, and sign the result. It is a

terrifying spectacle of human vanity which approaches madness...".

This diatribe, with its pointed reference to the presence of a woman painter in the group, illustrates the general reaction to the Impressionist's second attempt to exhibit their works. After the negative response to the 1874 exhibition, the press resorted to the scathing denigration of a

Claude MONET: *The Promenade (Woman with Umbrella).* The National Gallery of Art, Mellon Collection, Washington, DC.
By an audacious use of space and perspective, Monet transformed an ephemeral moment in to an unforgettable masterpiece of Impressionist art.

movement which was attempting to affirm its existence.

The second exhibition united approximately twenty artists, most of whom had taken part in the first, with the addition of newcomers like François and Tillot, old friends like Legros, and sympathizers such as Millet and Desboutin.

Millet's presence was practically fortuitous. His only connection to the group was his role as a naturalist precursor. Desboutin was a curious figure, who according to Zola, "was an Impressionist in the deepest sense of the word." After becoming penniless, he continued his joyous and bohemian existence among his artist friends (he appears in *The Absinthe Drinker* by Degas). Although a talented print-maker, he participated in the Second

Alfred SISLEY: *The Water-Trough at Marly in Winter.* The National Gallery, London.
Sisley was often inspired by scenes taken from the area in which he lived.

Impressionist Exhibition with a series of paintings. Caillebotte, whose energy and aid would be invaluable in the organization of exhibitions in the coming years, was another important and new member of the group, which now included Degas, Morisot, Pissarro, Renoir, Monet and Sisley. When considered along with secondary painters such as Béliard, Cals, Lepic, Levert, Ottin and Rouart, the membership was diverse enough to engender a certain amount of confusion concerning its artistic identity, while offering an easy target for ridicule by the press. The publication of *La Nouvelle Peinture* by Duranty indicated the prestige that the Impressionists had gradually acquired among the more enlightened members of the general public and the art critics; by

of opinion. The differences between *Portraits dans un bureau à La Nouvelle Orléans (Portraits in an Office in New Orleans)* by Degas, the fluid brushwork of Berthe Morisot's *Au bal (At the Ball)* and the intense luminosity of Monet's paintings of Argenteuil were more superficial than fundamental.

Geographical differences also began to appear within the group.

organizing the exhibition, Durand-Ruel provided a respectable showcase for the new aesthetic.

As each artist affirmed his style, the apparent homogeneity of the movement began to fluctuate, influenced more by temperament and experience than any real divergence

Camille PISSARRO: *Snow on the Slopes of Hermitage Hills*. Private Collection.
Pissarro shared Sisley's fascination with the ordinary details of daily life.

Financial considerations had caused some of its members to leave Paris for the nearby villages that ringed its periphery. Sisley, who had moved to Marly-le-Roi (2 avenue de l'Abreuvoir) in 1875, began to portray the neighboring landscapes in paintings such as *Avenue de l'Abreuvoir, Effet de neige, Une Route aux environs de Marly, Route de Saint-Germain* and *Inondation à Port-Marly (Flood at Port-Marly).*

The subjects beautifully represented the subtle alternating effects of sky and water. As was often the custom with the Impressionists (particularly Monet, in his series of *Meules [Haystacks]* and views of the Cathédrale of Rouen), Sisley painted no less than six versions of the flood at Port-Marly.

Although located in the

Claude MONET: *The Seine at Argenteuil.* Orsay Museum, Paris.
Although constantly evolving, Impressionism was particularly attentive to even the most prosaic aspects of existence. All the complexity of modern society was prefigured in its works.

geographical center of Versailles, Saint-Germain, Marly and Sèvres, a region whose beauty had already inspired so many early painters, Sisley's manner was anything but a return to the past. Historical vestiges were represented with the same contemporary style that Sisley reserved for his scenes of contemporary life in Paris, where he had set up his easel along the Canal Saint-Martin and captured all of its bustling activity. At Marly, he painted the docks along the Seine, expressing both their venerable past and recent economic dynamism. Rather than an exercise in nostalgia, he rendered the scene as a spontaneous impression of the present moment.

Ever the traveler, Sisley had early followed the urban exodus of the

in Montmartre and at 9 rue de la Paix (today rue La Condamine) in Batignolles with Bazille. In 1870, the effects of the Franco-Prussian War left him financially ruined. Abandoning his house in Bougival, he began living in the villages to the west of Paris, painting landscapes filled with a grave and tender serenity. His brushwork was precise and expressive, harmoniously rendering the

young artists who had revolted against the stultifying confinement of the Atelier Gleyre. A network of long-established friendships existed between his fellow-painters and his own father, of whom Renoir painted the portrait. Sisley himself appears in Renoir's *L'Auberge de la mère Anthony (Mother Anthony's Inn)*.

He had lived at 27 Cité des Fleurs

Alfred SISLEY: *Flood at Port-Marly.* Orsay Museum, Paris.
Even exceptional events served as subjects for the Impressionists, especially when connected to nature. But contrary to Romantic art which accentuated the dramatic aspects, Impressionism captured the subtle, furtive quality of such scenes.

luminosity of the sky and the earth marked by the changing seasons.

He developed his style in England before settling in Marly. In his incessant travels, complicated by family problems and financial difficulties, he progressively created an aesthetic approach which more than that of any other artist of the group (with the exception of Pissarro) would characterize Impressionism in its essence. Although his subjects appeared within their respective social contexts and were realistically portrayed, his work - particularly his treatment of water - had a distinctive dreamy quality, much like Monet's wintry, snow-filled compositions.

The Impressionist representation of nature and the elements rarely portrayed their violent aspects, contrary to Romanticism, which often

Gustave CAILLEBOTTE: *The Floor Sanders*. Orsay Museum, Paris.
The representation of the universe of work in painting corresponded to the emergence of the urban proletariat along with society's awareness of their struggles for dignity and the recognition of their basic rights. For an Impressionist artist, the humblest of workers was no less than a god of classical mythology.

accentuated their more dramatic qualities. Impressionism captured scenes in which the presence of man was nearly absent or at best, discreet: nature was portrayed as a force sufficient unto itself, existing in a timeless dimension.

Some artists, such as Lepic or Legros, participated in the movement without really belonging to it, drawn into the circle of Impressionism by their friendships with its painters. At the same time, the movement itself, suffering from a lack of uniform stylistic orientation, failed to appear as a cohesive entity in the eyes of the public, even as it attempted to establish its own limits and identity. The influence of Degas would be determinate, for he would gradually gain control of the exhibition and

would henceforth pass through them and they would establish its laws. Rather than attempting to become the stars of the movement, they focused it and gave it its populist orientation.

demand the inclusion of his friends.

Caillebotte would mark his difference with *The Floor Sanders*, while Renoir would render an implicit homage to Bazille, who had died and to whom all of the Impressionists had an artistic debt. Pissarro *(Snow on the Hills of the Hermitage; Snow at Louveciennes)* and Sisley defined the rules of the game: Impressionism

Edgar DEGAS: *Portraits in an Office in New Orleans*. Museum of Fine Arts. Pau, France.
No subject was unworthy of being represented by Impressionist artists: for them, painting was a manner of documenting the multiple facets of modern life.

Third Exhibition, 1877

More than any other member of the group, Cézanne had suffered from the intolerance of the Jury of the Salon and had all but given up hope of exhibiting his works alongside those of the artists who had gained the recognition of the public and its official institutions.

Although he took part in the First Impressionist Exhibition, he chose not to participate in the second. Quarrelsome and voluble, he rapidly marked his distance from certain artists belonging to the movement, such as Monet. In a letter to his friend Victor Chocquet, who would be one of his most faithful supporters, Cézanne flatly stated that "the exhibition (...) will be a failure if we have to show with Monet." It was a serious injustice on his part, for the latter artist had defended him against the criticisms of Lepic, who wanted to exclude him from the exhibition.

Although he had joined Zola in Paris in 1861, the situation was uncomfortable, and he passed through a succession of studios and temporary apartments in the years that followed. Finding himself

Gustave CAILLEBOTTE: *Paris Under the Rain*. Art Institute of Chicago. The city which had long been the showcase for the monarchy progressively accommodated the triumph of the bourgeoisie and its distinctive mannerisms.

married and with a family in 1872, he began a stable and fertile period in Pontoise and Auvers, thanks to Pissarro's support. Progressively, he became conscious of his objectives and the difficulties in attaining them. His ambitions were enormous, but at the same time he was handicapped by a terrible lack of self-confidence.

Constrained by finances, he found it necessary to live more economically. Leaving Paris, to which he had returned and where he had failed to find a satisfactory environment for his painting, he moved to l'Estaque in 1876. Once there, he invited his friends to share the incomparable luminosity of the region.

His participation in the Third Impressionist Exhibition which united only eighteen other artists "in an empty apartment on the second floor of a building at 6 rue Le Peletier on the same street as the Durand-Ruel galleries" would be his last. From that time on, he continued alone, pushing the limits of his art in directions that even his closest friends would consider with doubt and skepticism.

The works which appeared at the third exhibition consisted of still-lives, floral compositions, *Les Baigneurs (The Bathers)*, and figure studies. His paintings were criticized for what was considered to be the aggressiveness of his style. It was as if their new and provocative force had invalidated their existence, despite the authenticity of his manner and his concern for expressing the essence of his subjects.

An art critic of the period wrote that "Mr. Paul Cézanne is the most authentic of Impressionists. Each of the paintings shown on the rue Le Peletier is more incredible than the next. Above all, our attention was drawn to his study of a man's head, a work whose strangeness can only have been a deliberate choice. Above this portrait, Mr. Cézanne has placed his *Bathers,* rendered in dark sooty tones. It appears that this is only a preliminary study, but it is one that the artist would be well-advised not to carry any further." Another critic attacked his work even more violently, proclaiming that his paintings "were both laughable and lamentable, revealing the most total ignorance of line, composition and color."

Cézanne had already been the target of critics during the first exhibition in 1874, when Castagnary wrote the following diatribe: "If the others who visibly lack any thought or training concerning art have pushed their "Impressions" to outrageous limits, the example of Mr. Cézanne (particularly in his *Modern Olympia)* illustrates the destiny that surely awaits them. From idealization to idealization, they will arrive at this same excessive romanticism, in which nature is nothing more than the excuse for representing pure fantasy and where the imagination is incapable of expressing anything other than disjointed fantasies of subjective reality, escaping all connection to the real world and its logic."

Faced by such hostility and incomprehension, Cézanne totally abandoned an artistic arena which he neither cared for nor in which he desired to compete. His lack of self-confidence, the demands he placed upon his own art and a need for solitude made it necessary for him to retire from such battles. These conflicts would produce their share of heroes and martyrs, but Cézanne was in a class by himself and his destiny would be both sublime and cruel.

Closely allied with Monet, Pissarro, Renoir and Sisley contributed to the impression of continuity within the group. Degas, who exhibited his *Femme devant un café (Woman in Front of a Café)*, *Ecole de danse (The Dance School)* and *Cabinet de toilette (The Bathroom)*, was somewhat apart. Caillebotte, both by his subjects and his manner of representing them within a realistic psychological context, was similarly modern, but more reserved and concise. His magisterial *Rue de Paris, temps de pluie (Paris Street in the Rain)* and *Le Pont de l'Europe (The Europe Bridge)* are works whose high-pitched theatricality and modern style freed them from the constraints of the Academy and perfectly corresponded to the new aesthetics promoted by writers such as Zola and Huysmans.

Renoir's paintings were saturated with light and his universe soft, tender, heady and sensual, such as in *La Balançoire (The Swing)* and *Bal du Moulin de la Galette (The Ball at the Moulin de la Galette).* His choice of subjects was extremely diverse (Hoschedé's command for the Chateau of Montgeron had sparked *Marly - The Machine at Marly, Le Pont d'Argenteuil - Argenteuil Bridge)* continued in their tender manner, sensitive to the slightest nuances of light and often portraying scenes of banal contemporary reality and the transformations imposed by progress. All of this left Cézanne indifferent, absorbed in the goal of expressing the eternal aspects of temporal existence.

his interest in the Saint-Lazare railway station and contemporary views of Paris) and illustrated the full scope of his talent and the breadth of an always-renewed artistic vision.

Both Pissarro *(Bords de l'Oise - On the Banks of the Oise; route d'Auvers - The Auvers Road; La Plaine à Pontoise - The Plain of Pontoise)* and Sisley *(La Machine à*

Edgar DEGAS: *The Dance Class.* The Corcoran Gallery of Art, Washington, DC.

In Paris during the latter half of the nineteenth century attending performances at the opera was a vital social ritual of the upper-middle classes. There, Degas frequented Halévy, the author of *The Cardinal Family,* the literary counterpart of his paintings, which so lucidly revealed the strangely ambiguous world of the theater.

Fourth Exhibition, 1879

A tireless spectator of life and amusements in the lower-class neighborhoods of Paris, Degas also haunted the backstage and rehearsal rooms of the Opera, observing and painting the participants of a world at once bourgeois and bohemian that Halévy described with humor and stinging irony in *La Famille Cardinal*.

Degas was basically the eyes of his generation. Open-minded and inquisitive, following the movements of the dancers like a hawk, he noted the contrasting cadences of the dark-clad males and the ethereal grace of the young ballerinas during rehearsals. Goncourt related one of these backstage visits in his *Journal:* "When Degas portrays the seamstresses, it is as if we are there in front of them, hearing them speak and explaining their technique of ironing the costumes.... Next, the line of dancers appears, where the natural luminosity of the window backlights the amazing silhouettes of their legs as they descend the tiny stairway in the brilliant splash of the red plaid of their jackets and the vaporous clouds of their skirts... ."

His participation in the Fourth Impressionist Exhibition *(Miss Lola at the Circus, Portrait of Duranty, Washerwomen Carrying Laundry,* the astonishing *Café Singer* and many representations of classical dancers) corresponded to the emergence of a "naturalist" current, accentuated by the absence of Renoir, Sisley, Cézanne and Berthe Morisot.

The diversity of his choice of subjects in no way diminished the precision of his manner of portraying them. This was evident not only in the authenticity of the gestures of his ballerinas and in the documentary quality of the scenes of wardrobe-mistresses and their assistants, but

Edgar DEGAS: *Miss Lola at the Circus.* The National Gallery, London. Like the café-concerts, the circus fascinated painters such as Degas, Seurat and, later, Toulouse-Lautrec.

Edgar DEGAS: *The Café Singer (Singer with Glove)*. Fogg Art Museum, Harvard University, Cambridge (MA).
As if to compensate for his inability to reproduce the woman's song, Degas accentuated the power and dramatic quality of the gestures which accompanied it.

Mary CASSATT: *Woman Reading*.
Joslyn Art Museum, Omaha
(Nebraska).
Much can be read into scenes such as
this, representing the rituals and habits
of the French bourgeoisie in the latter
half of the nineteenth century.

also in his portrayal of the urban environment to which he was particularly attached. "He is developing an entirely new style of painting" said a critic of the period. Since the creation of the group and the first exhibition at Nadar's studio, Degas had united a circle of artists (such as Lepic, De Nittis, Zandomeneghi and Forain) whose work he admired and which

It was during this period that Degas moved out of his lodgings at 77 rue Blanche and on the same day moved into what he described as "the most marvelous apartment and studio that one could imagine. It is as if it had directly materialized from all that one had dreamed of: a small two-story house overlooking the most astonishing scenes...and all of them right in front of my door, between the

validated his own aesthetic choices.

Those who, like Cézanne, abandoned the group were often motivated by the hope of exhibiting at the Salon or, like Renoir, actually did so. They heightened the potential for dissension within the movement. Monet, whose works were abundantly represented, regretted that such conflicts disturbed the cohesion of the group.

Claude MONET: *Terrace at Sainte-Adresse*. The Metropolitan Museum of Art, New York.
The painting expresses the somewhat pinched charm of the Parisian salon transposed to a sea-side resort where the art of polite conversation was carried on despite the radical change in the surroundings.

rue de Laval and Place Pigalle."

He began multiplying his sketches of street scenes and reading Muydbridge's theories in *The Motion of the Horse* which analyzed the movements of a horse's legs at a gallop. Degas, who frequently attended horse races, was particularly attentive to its findings.

By the scope of his manner and the modernity, daring and impudent realism of his subjects, Degas was at the heart of the contradictions of Impressionism. Of all the painters of the movement, he was the closest in spirit both to writers such as Zola, Alexis, Maupassant and Huysmans who propounded the aesthetic of naturalism, and to the cause of open-air painting practiced by his fellow-artists.

More than anyone else, J.K. Huysmans appreciated his

Gustave CAILLEBOTTE: *The Canoers.* The National Gallery of Art, Washington, DC.
Born of the moment in all its spontaneity, Impressionist art attempted to capture action even as it occurred.

talent: "Degas is the master of the art of portraying women, representing their charming movements and gracious attitudes, whatever the class of society to which they belong."

It was with one of his favorite themes that he produced one of his most audaciously modern works, *The Café Singer.* The "café-concerts" which occupied an ambiguous position between lower-class amusement and a social activity for the Parisian bourgeoisie, were frequented by a mixed crowd of all social and economic categories. Degas, a bachelor and avid curiosity-seeker, often attended such events, drawn to them much in the same way as to the intimate backstage scenes at the Opera, concert-halls, the stock market and bordellos that so fascinated him and which inspired

According to a writer of the period, everything in the solitary and profoundly misogynous life of Degas was nothing more than a "long moment of vanity, order and good behavior: all of those estimable virtues which typify the perfect provincial civil servant."

Despite their authenticity and profound sense of psychological observation, his works were the

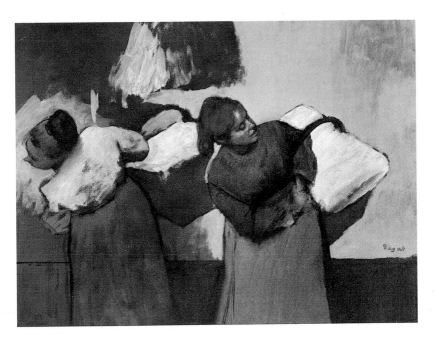

sketches whose sharp realism mirrored the universe of Maupassant or of that depicted by Huysmans in his novel *Martha, the Story of a Prostitute.*

By his portrayal of these seldom-represented scenes, Degas revealed a hidden world of innate violence, sensuality and voluptuousness, where masks and artificiality dissolved in the assaults of desire and exhaustion.

Edgar DEGAS: *Washerwomen Carrying Laundry.* Private Collection.
Nearly palpable, the woman's' effort is translated into the lines of her body.

paradoxical reflection of the inherent social distance between an artist portraying scenes and the distaste of a member of the bourgeoisie observing the lower classes.

If, as according to Gustave Coquiot, Degas represented women as if they were biological specimens in a clinical study, it is certain that they were far-removed from the brilliant nudes of Renoir, with their creamy skin and gestures recalling those of ancient priestesses offering wine and flowers to the divinities of the earth. Degas portrayed his Venuses in the seamy atmosphere of servants' rooms, with one leg hoisted over the edge of a zinc bathing-tub filled with dirty water. Their gestures were purely a question of personal hygiene and their bodies were less representations of sensuality than ananatomical study of flesh, muscles and sweat.

The constant attraction exercised by the official Salon on young painters who believed (or knew) that its prestige was a necessary step in their career, deprived the Impressionist exhibition of some of its most gifted artists, such as Renoir, who was accepted by the jury of the Salon even as Sisley was rejected. The Bracquemonds presented several of their works, as did Cals and Charles Tillot. The presence of Zandomeneghi, Forain and Mary Cassatt was due to the influence of Degas. Mary Cassatt was a newcomer who had been discovered by Degas and who posed for him in *Chez la modiste (At the Dressmaker's)*. Degas encouraged her as a painter, progressively developing her self-confidence, originality and audacity. She repaid his efforts in paintings such as *Femme dans une loge (Woman in a Theater-Box)* and *Femme lisant (Woman Reading)*, executed in her forthright and energetic manner in light and lively colors.

A posthumous homage was paid to Ludovic Piette, who had participated in the third exhibition thanks to the influence of his friend and sometime neighbor in Pontoise, Pissarro. Piette's manner was slightly more sentimental and populist, qualities which made him more acceptable to a public leery of any form of stylistic or thematic innovation.

Recruited by Degas, Forain exhibited works dealing with Parisian life, a subject in which he excelled. Forain was also a brilliant member of the circle of artists and writers that gravitated around Nina de Callias and an intimate of Verlaine and Rimbaud. He was particularly close to the latter poet, who lived in his studio on the rue Campagne-Première during the period that Fantin-Latour painted *Around the Table*. Forain, who frequented both the gutters and the glitterati of Paris, was similar to Degas but expressed an even more energetic and focused vision of existence in his works.

The fourth exhibition provided the opportunity for J.K. Huysmans to involve himself even further on the side of the Impressionists. After visiting the official Salon, he noted that "I have often been astonished by the effect upon art produced by the Impressionists and writers such as Flaubert, Goncourt and Zola. They have revealed Naturalism to the public and forever transformed the conception of art, freeing it from the constraints of the establishment and its schools." It is significant that Huysmans placed art and literature on the same level, while positing Naturalism and Impressionism as two manners of expressing an identical vision of reality.

Caillebotte's works were the perfect illustration of this apparent dichotomy. He showed paintings such as *Canotiers (The Canoers)*, *Partie de bateaux (Boating)* and *Périssoires (Sculls)*, inspired by his passion for boating and the memories of the years spent as a young man on his parents' estate in Yerres, as well as several intensely personal cityscapes of Paris. *Vue des toits, effet de neige*

A native of Normandy, he was a member of the local movement of open-air painters which included Boudin. Fascinated by natural light, Lebourg perfected his style and enlarged the chromatic range of his palette in Algeria, where he worked as a teacher. His works are part of the Impressionist current exemplified by Jongkind and Dupré, both of whom had chosen to abandon the studio for the reality of the exterior world.

(Roofs and Snow) and *Rue Halévy, vue du sixième étage (View From the Sixth Floor of rue Halévy)*, possessed a unique photographic quality all their own.

Among the other artists at the fourth exhibition was Albert Lebourg.

Gustave CAILLEBOTTE: *View Over the Roofs with Snow*. Orsay Museum, Paris.
The elements, particularly rain or snow, both in the country and in an urban context, fascinated many of the Impressionist painters. Here, it is expressed with an exquisite subtlety that speaks of solitude, the passage of time and a certain atmosphere of mystery.

Fifth Exhibition, 1880

The Fifth Impressionist Exhibition, held at 10 rue des Pyramides, was marked by the absence of many of the most important members of the movement, including Monet, Renoir, Sisley and Cézanne. The presence of Raffaëlli, encouraged to exhibit by his friend Degas, only confirmed the decision of those who had chosen to withdraw, for they considered his works as more or less skillful adaptations of the Impressionist spirit, but essentially based upon anecdotal themes and popular realism occasionally touched by *miserabilism*. Huysmans enthusiastically described his manner as follows: "Imagine one of those dark, gray days when the clouds race and collide across the immense and somber sky. The pale earth stretches away under the dreary light; in the distance, the tops of poplar trees sway under the force of the wind, as if whipping the rain-filled clouds rolling above a sad cottage abandoned in the middle of a deserted plain..." .

Impressionists such as Monet and Renoir who had succeeded in being accepted by the jury of the Salon nevertheless found themselves under attack by the critics. They reacted by asking Zola, whom they considered as a friend and sympathizer, to defend their cause. The result was his *Le Naturalisme au Salon (Naturalism at the Salon)*, which was less an apology of

Félix BRACQUEMOND: *Portrait of Edmond de Goncourt*. Louvre Museum, Paris.
Although unlike Zola or Huysmans, Edmond de Goncourt never commented upon the emergence of Impressionism in his writings, he was nevertheless a friend of many of the movement's most talented artists.

Marie BRACQUEMOND: *Woman in White*. Municipal Museum of Cambrai, France.
When the art of the portrait was in the hands of women, the result was no different than that executed by male artists, as if the style of expression was determined by the model portrayed.

Berthe MORISOT: *Summer*. Fabre
Museum, Montpellier, France.
The gentle disarray of the woman's
garments expresses the pleasure of the
open air and the miracle of the secret
influences of the environment upon all
human beings.

Impressionism than a further and pointed criticism of the movement itself: "It is extremely unfortunate that there is not a single artist in this group who definitively exemplifies the new style that all of them employ to varying degrees in their works. The formula is there, but so fragmented that it is nowhere totally present, for none of them have entirely mastered it. They are merely precursors; the

wishes to say." It was apparent that Zola, like Huysmans, was incapable of defending works which did not conform to his own vision of the world.

Caillebotte was one of the most original personalities of the group and his work reflected this special uniqueness. He had actively contributed to the organization of the fifth exhibition, in which he included

real genius hasn't even been born yet. It's clear what they are trying to do, and they are right to do it, but there is no masterpiece that exemplifies their movement (...) And that is why the Impressionists have so far failed in their struggle for recognition: they are inferior to the task they are attempting to accomplish, like someone stuttering without being able to pronounce the word he

Berthe MORISOT: *Young Girl at Her Dressing Table.* Art Institute of Chicago. The frequently-repeated subject of women in the intimacy of their homes expresses the general conceptions concerning their essence during the latter half of the nineteenth century. It is instructive to compare the present work with the brittle cynicism of Manet's *Nana.*

a series of strikingly contemporary paintings such as *Dans un café (In a Café)* and *Vue prise à travers un balcon (View From a Balcony)*, portraying scenes of ordinary life. They revealed all of the distance existing between artists like Raffaëlli or Zandomeneghi who relied on anecdotal material and Caillebotte's manner which was so innovative as to be practically a re-invention of painting itself.

By its audacity and force of expression, *View From a Balcony* focused on a reality that none of the other painters of the movement had even attempted to express. Caillebotte's scenes of the Parisian streets and their bustling activity were often marked by an impression of solitude which would progressively emerge in the works of other period artists. Mary Cassatt's works were bathed in a charming atmosphere of warm femininity. A close friend of Degas, and reflecting the same bourgeois vision of middle-class existence as he, she nevertheless lacked his energy and underlying virulence. As a female painter and by her aesthetic orientation, she was doubly handicapped in relation to the art establishment of the period. Although impeccably rendered, her habitually restrained choice of subjects - essentially representations of mothers with their children and intimate scenes of family life - were considered as being too aesthetically advanced by the official jury of the Salon.

Even if the participation of the Bracquemonds was limited to a modest selection of engravings and ceramics, these works reflected the penetration of Impressionism in media other than painting. The quality of Felix Bracquemond's engravings had established him as an authentic artist and attracted the interest of the poet Baudelaire, who in turn introduced him into the literary circle frequented by writers like Banville, Barbey d'Aurevilly and Philippe Burty. Bracquemond was also a regular of the Nouvelle-Athènes and a friend of Manet, Degas and Fantin-Latour, who portrayed him in his *Hommage à Delacroix (Homage to Delacroix)*. With Degas, Pissarro and Mary Cassatt, he developed the project of publishing *Le Jour et la nuit (Day and Night)*, a magazine devoted to engravings.

The Portrait of Edmond de Goncourt was an icon-like and passionate work which portrayed the writer amidst the objects of his collection, obviously satisfied with himself and the position he occupied in the Parisian world of arts and letters. Goncourt's connection with Impressionism was tenuous, despite his early exposure to the movement through Renoir, who had been his neighbor during the period when it was beginning to gather momentum. Bracquemond's wife Marie - who had frequented Manet's studio - represented intimate scenes of family life in works like *Sous la lampe (Under the Lamp)* and *Femme à l'ombrelle (Woman with Umbrella)*, echoes of the visits of the Sisleys to her home in Sèvres.

Levert, who had been introduced into the group by Degas and who had already shown in the first exhibition, was a fairly conventional but accomplished landscape painter whose sensitivity to nature was apparent in works like *Bords de l'Essonne (On the Banks of the Essonne)*, *Etude à Malesherbes (Study at Malesherbes)* and *Plaine de la Brie (The Plain of the Brie)*. Just as he was fading from the movement - for the fifth exhibition would be the last time he exhibited with the Impressionists - Eugène Vidal's star began to rise. Although Armand Silvestre judged paintings such as *Portrait of George Sand, Femme en blanc (Woman in White)* and *Au café (At the Café)* as sufficient proof of his talent as a painter, Vidal's contribution to the movement - like those of Vignon, Levert and Tillot - can be considered as being of minor importance.

Henri ROUART : *Terrace on the Banks of the Seine at Melun*. Orsay Museum, Paris.
Rouart's paintings were like a personal diary of his own experiences, in which he documented the charms and beauty of his life and immediate environment.

Sixth Exhibition, 1881

Edgar DEGAS: *Cabaret*. Corcoran Gallery of Art, Washington, DC. A tireless visitor of Paris by night and a regular at the city's bars and cabarets, Degas often expressed his underlying misogyny in his representations of women as simple objects of pleasure. The painter's vision is an uncompromising and pitiless confrontation with hidden aspects of reality.

The Sixth Impressionist Exhibition was marked by a schism between the ongoing current of naturalism exercised by Degas and his followers and a small group of painters whose works lacked both the excellence and aesthetic rigor of the mainstream Impressionists. Whether by pure chance or by a deliberate and highly symbolic choice, the exhibition was held at 35 boulevard des Capucines, in the same building as the first exhibition seven years earlier.

The seven years had been accompanied by a series of quarrels and internal dissension that had progressively undermined the cohesion of the movement which had painstakingly emerged despite the widely different stylistic and aesthetic orientations of its participants.

Caillebotte, who had invested so much energy in the organization of the preceding exhibition, was absent; other desisting artists included Renoir, Monet, Sisley and Cézanne. The result was damaging to the image of Impressionism as a movement. One positive effect was that the critics and public suddenly became more tolerant; it was as if the absence of the principal targets no

longer justified the energy usually deployed to attack them. As for the other participating artists, which included Jean Louis Forain, Zandomeneghi and Raffaëlli, there was little to criticize; since they were less threatening in their approach, styles and aesthetics, they were more readily accepted. Huysmans, appraising Raffaëlli's work, wrote: "Among the numerous painters of our epoch, I am certain that Raffaëlli is one of the few who will endure; he will obtain a privileged position in the art of this century, that of a Parisian Millet...".

Jean-François RAFFAELLI: *The Absinthe Drinkers*. Private Collection. A picturesque treatment of a subject frequently painted by his contemporaries. The fascination of the scene dominates the purely pictorial aspects of the work.

Guillaumin, who had appeared in the first, third and all of the subsequent exhibitions, painted the industrial landscapes of the suburbs of Paris and naturalist scenes within the capital itself. Works like *Quai des Célestins, Quai de la Rapée* and *Quai d'Austerlitz* expressed banal, unadorned reality rather than an idealized vision of existence.

Pissarro provided numerous works for the sixth exhibition, faithful in his ways and among the few artists of the original group who had not modified or transformed his style during the years that followed the first exhibition. He was a painter who was totally committed to the representation of everyday reality, expressed in soft, low-key colors with an inoffensive manner that preserved him from the criticism directed at many of his fellow-painters. Like many of them, he had left France for England during the Franco-Prussian War in 1870. And, as for many of these artists, the experience had been artistically enriching. Pissarro had been born in the French Caribbean in 1830; after arriving in Paris, he successively lived at 49 rue Notre-Dame-de-Lorette (1856), 38-bis rue Fontaine (1859), 39 rue de Douai (1860), 23 rue Bréda (1862) and 108 boulevard de Rochechouart (1866). After this restless period, he settled in the nearby village of Pontoise (rue de l'Hermitage) whose surroundings would become one of his principal sources of inspiration: *La Sente aux choux (The Cabbage Path), Paysage pris sur le vieux chemin d'Ennery-Pontoise (Landscape on the Old Ennery-Pontoise Road).* He also set up his easel in and around Louveciennes (1869); the series of paintings which resulted are marked by a persistent melancholy.

Pissarro was deeply influenced by the places in which he chose to live. Their atmosphere and personality was generally reflected in his works through an effect of symbiosis which gave his paintings their particularly seductive sense of intimacy. He was also attracted to the common people of the countryside, their way of life seemingly unchanged for centuries. Pissarro's populist sympathies were expressed in a peaceful and unostentatious manner, at opposite ends from that of Courbet, who generally militated for specific causes through his art.

In his life as much as in his painting, Pissarro's approach was basically conciliatory. In addition to his efforts to reduce the dissension and conflicts among his fellow-Impressionists he also encouraged artists such as Cézanne, selflessly providing moral and even financial support.

After mastering the expression of a new and humanistic vision of peasant life in his works, Pissarro's painting progressively became even more socially engaged. His themes were enriched by the representation of individuals who were the products of the continuous transformation of society in the latter half of the nineteenth century, changes which had altered the existence of the peasant classes and created the urban proletariat.

Like Pissarro, Berthe Morisot's firm social commitment was reflected in her work. She was also one of the group's most faithful members, participating in all of their exhibitions except the third in 1877. Sensitive and feminine, she needed the collective energy of a movement to overcome the prejudices weighing upon any woman who dared abandon her predestined role as a homemaker for a career as an artist.

She began painting early, encouraged by her family and the guidance of friends like Fantin-Latour and Manet, whom she seduced while sitting for what would prove to be some of his best portraits. Mallarmé, who was also among her admirers, would surpass himself in the prose he employed to describe the quality of her work. Her modest contribution to the sixth exhibition - *Etude de plein air (Open-Air Study), Nourrice et bébé (Wet Nurse and Baby), Jeune Femme en rose (Young Woman in Pink), Portrait d'enfant (Portrait of a Child)* -was the visible proof that she had found the tone, rhythm and specific approach to her art.

Calm, intelligent and attentive to her family (she eventually married Manet's brother Eugène), her comfortably bourgeois domestic life

Berthe MORISOT: *Wet Nurse and Baby*. Private Collection.
Delighted by motherhood, Berthe Morisot frequently painted scenes expressive of the maternal instinct in which she captured the touching fragility of an existence totally dependant upon the care of those responsible for protecting and nurturing it.

provided the necessary foundation for the sensitively emotional type of painting she practiced. Harmonious and serene, it was like an intimate personal diary of her life as a wife, mother and hostess to the select circle of artists and writers who were her friends.

The experience of motherhood greatly affected both her life and her painting. The birth of her daughter Julie in 1878 had a determinate effect upon her work, both nourishing and sharpening her vision. Like her mother, Julie was surrounded by an exceptional group of artists and writers; Degas, Renoir and Mallarmé were her familiars in a household free of material constraints and open to the newest intellectual currents of the period. To this cultural environment of exceptional quality was added an

Camille PISSARRO: *Country Lane and Cabbage Fields*. Museum of the Chartreuse. Douai, France.
From painting to painting, Pissarro documented his rural environment, representing humble scenes of peasant life, whose traditional wisdom he admired.

education which produced an equally exceptional young woman whose rich inner life was revealed in her diaries. In a period where diaries often expressed thoughts which could never be openly avowed, Julie's writings were filled with astonishingly lucid observations of the uncommon personalities that visited her family and who progressively influenced the development of her own personality.

Federico ZANDOMENEGHI: *Place d'Anvers*. Galleria d'Arte Moderna Ricci Oddi. Piacenza, Italy.
An urban variation on the theme of the pleasures of the open air, replete with children and their nurses.

Seventh Exhibition, 1882

Pierre-Auguste Renoir: *Young Woman with Cat*. Sterling and Francine Clark Art Institute, Williamstown (MA).
In earlier periods, the woman would have been portrayed as a classical goddess. Although she expresses the same sensual beauty, her peasant origins are clearly revealed. The resulting portrait is both familiar and compelling.

In the latter half of the 1870s, Renoir had enlarged the circle of his social relations and was often commissioned to execute light and joyous portraits such as *Madame Charpentier*.

His studio was located on the high floor of a building facing the busy Pont-Neuf, which he occasionally chose as a subject. His range widened, alternating between the formalism of posed portraits and the rapid brushwork of street scenes. He had painted side by side with Monet in his garden in Argenteuil and in the vicinity, capturing fleeting moments of the play of light upon water, leaves and vegetation. While maintaining his residence on the rue Saint-Georges, he had moved from studio to studio in the neighborhood before choosing the one on rue Cortot. It was the period of the deliciously exuberant floral studies such as *Le Jardin de la rue Cortot (The Garden of the rue Cortot)*, which he used to highlight the blond and voluptuous beauty of the nudes portrayed in *Baigneuses (The Bathers)*. Along with the intimate vision of *Monet peignant dans son jardin à Argenteuil (Monet Painting in his Garden in Argenteuil)* and the opulent atmosphere of *La Loge (The Theater Box)*, there were also works like *Les Amoureux (The Lovers)*, whose romantic sentimentality were like illustrations from the pages of Alphonse Daudet's novels. Later, following a voyage through Italy, Renoir would speak of his "old masters" in reference to the great classical painters of the peninsula.

Although he had refused to participate in the Seventh Impressionist Exhibition - explaining his absence by his presence at the Salon the same year - a series of Renoir's works was included by

Durand-Ruel, who had rented space in the Panorama of Reischoffen to present paintings selected from his personal collection. Renoir's *Jeune Fille au chat (Young Girl and Cat), Une Loge à l'Opéra (A Private Box at the Opera), Un Déjeuner à Bougival (Luncheon at Bougival), La Seine à Chatou (The Seine at Chatou)* and more recent works inspired by his visit to Algeria *(Jardin Desaix à Alger - The Desaix Garden in Algiers)* were thus part of the exhibition.

The absence of Degas, compensated by the presence of his followers, re-oriented the exhibition back to the tradition of open-air painting and attracted the participation of artists such as Monet and Sisley, who had previously deserted it to explore other horizons. If the current of naturalism had finally been neutralized, a new and highly individualistic artistic vision emerged onto the scene: that of Gauguin.

Gauguin had entered the

Paul GAUGUIN: *Dreaming Child.* Ordrupgaard Sammlungen, Copenhagen.
Before attaining the authentically revolutionary level of his art, Gauguin's approach to painting was marked by humility, visible here in his expression of the miracle of life and the tender beauty of youth.

Impressionist movement by the back door. He had participated in the fourth exhibition in 1879, but so discreetly that his name never appeared in the catalogue. He had also lent the exhibition three paintings by Pissarro, which placed him in the ambiguous position of participating both as a painter and a collector.

Gauguin was at that time little more than a talented "amateur" painter working as a bank clerk and living a conventional bourgeois existence. His salary had permitted him to move from his apartment on Place Saint-Georges and the neighborhood in which he had been born (on the nearby rue Notre-Dame-de-Lorette) to more luxurious lodgings near the Trocadero. But financial difficulties soon forced the family to move to a more modest

Paul GAUGUIN: *Still-Life with Flowers*. National Gallery, Oslo.
All of the elements of an intimate approach to art (the piano, flowers and the peaceful atmosphere of home) are united in this work. Although in contact with the Impressionists and frequently representing the same subjects in his early period, Gauguin progressively developed a totally different style.

apartment at 74 rue des Fourneaux.

Gauguin's decision to devote himself entirely to painting despite the opposition of his wife and in-laws was accompanied by the abandonment of his job at the bank. Symbolically speaking, it was as if his choice to be an artist literally excluded the possibility of both a regular salary and the comfortable middle-class existence that went with it.

Pierre-Auguste RENOIR: *The Lovers*.
Narodni Galeri v Praze, Prague.
Adam and Eve in period costumes,
inhabiting Paradise regained. There is
no need to fear the wrath of God here,
since for the moment, He is visibly
absent.

Motivated by an irrepressible desire to express himself through art, Gauguin frequented the Impressionist painters who regularly gathered at the Nouvelle-Athènes café. His presence went largely unnoticed, which given his impulsive and rather authoritarian personality, indicated how much respect and humility he could muster when in the presence of what he considered to be authentic artists.

Gauguin's respect for artists in general and the painters whose works he collected in particular was rewarded by his acceptance by the jury of the Salon, even as Manet and Cézanne were being rejected. His participation in both exhibitions violated one of the long-standing principles of the Impressionists, which forbade an artist showing in their exhibition from participating in an official Salon. This rule would create numerous conflicts during the years of the Impressionist exhibitions, and Gauguin's example only accentuated the underlying dissension that had accumulated within the movement and which terminated in the defection of Cézanne and the final participation by Sisley and Renoir.

When he exhibited at the fifth exhibition, Gauguin was still under the influence of Pissarro, whom he had joined in Pontoise. His capacities of assimilation and synthesis were astonishing: in the progressive development of his own style he would transcend all of the artists who had influenced him. He arrived in Pont-Aven at the very moment that the Impressionists had definitively disbanded as a group. His participation in the sixth exhibition revealed the progress he had made, even if the works were still marked by the uncertainty that resulted from his financial situation and the highly-critical attitude of his wife Mette, who would separate from him after a trip to her native Denmark.

One of his most remarkable works in the seventh exhibition was *Fleurs, nature morte (Still-Life with Flowers)*, which Huysmans described as "dark and obsessive." The scene portrayed a conventional interior with a woman seated at a piano and a man watching her play. A huge bouquet of flowers in the foreground provided the inspiration for the title of the work, which in the manner of Degas was an expression of the stultifying atmosphere of bourgeois life. Gauguin's vision was both tender and cynical, touched by the impatience with the superficial of an apprentice artist painfully learning his craft and developing his style. As a late-comer to the movement and more or less a new artist, Gauguin had to work twice as hard for recognition as his fellow-painters who had already established themselves through repeated exhibitions either with the Impressionists or in the official Salons. And despite the lack of encouragement and support of these same artists, he would invest an immense effort to raise himself to their level of experience and professionalism.

Given the defection of certain artists and the reticence of still others, the seventh exhibition was difficult to organize. If it took place at all, it was above all due to the dedication of Durand-Ruel. Paradoxically, the exhibition was among the most aesthetically homogeneous of all, including the first, for it drew upon the best elements of the movement, including works by Caillebotte, Guillaumin, Monet, Morisot, Pissarro, Renoir and Sisley. At the same time, the artists of lesser quality - particularly those who had attracted the scorn of the critics in the preceding exhibitions - were absent.

Vignon exhibited, as he had done since 1880. He had studied under Cals (who had discreetly participated in the early exhibitions) and painted in the same region as Pissarro, whom he encountered in and around Pontoise, as well as in places frequented by Cézanne and Guillaumin. He also was a friend of Van Gogh, whom he greatly admired and considered joining in Arles, as would Gauguin.

Degas was fittingly absent from the seventh exhibition: it was he and the artists who emulated him who had for years contributed to the dissension within the movement, undermining its commitment to a spontaneous art of open-air painting that celebrated the beauty of nature.

Pierre-Auguste RENOIR: *The Desaix Garden in Algiers*. Private Collection. Renoir was attracted to the Mediterranean region by its special luminosity, more intense than that of the Ile-de-France. He captured its sensual voluptuousness in his works, whereas Cézanne only expressed its harsh clarity.

Eighth Exhibition, 1886

The death of Manet in 1883 was a blow to his friends and the numerous artists who admired or emulated his style. His disciple Eva Gonzalès was so stricken that she died several days after learning of Manet's demise; it was as if Impressionism had been decapitated, deprived of the one artist who had always guided its movements, justified its choices, and participated in all of its struggles.

A page in the movement's history had been turned, which paradoxically would liberate its members from the internal conflicts that had plagued it from the beginning.

Many of the artists who entered the movement at its origin had since achieved recognition, aided by the dynamism of Durand-Ruel who had done his utmost to promote them. He had also begun to reap the first rewards of his investment, for the prices of the works of the artists he had defended, ridiculously low during the 1875 sale, had progressively risen to comfortable levels. The 1882 exhibition had been organized along the lines of a veritable marketing campaign. The commercial objectives had been established by Durand-Ruel and the quality of the works more than fulfilled his expectations.

The difference between the seventh and eighth exhibitions illustrated this situation. The awareness of the futility of fighting a battle which was partially won, and the diverging careers of those who had participated for so many years in the combat, made any confrontation meaningless.

Even Pissarro, who had been one of the most orthodox Impressionists, began to abandon the principles which were its foundation. En 1882, after moving to the village of Eragny-

Paul GAUGUIN: *The Pond*. Civica Galleria d'Arte Moderna, Milan. Gauguin's works progressively reveal the emergence of a new trend within the Impressionist movement and announce the entirely different direction his painting would take in the near future.

sur-Epte near Gisors, henceforth his home-base, his art began to reflect the influence of Pointillism, which would increasingly be projected to the forefront after the creation of the *Salon des Indépendants*.

Like Impressionism, Pointillism had been subjected to the ostracism of the official art establishment. The severity of the juries in 1883 and 1884 toward the new movement of artists

had resulted in their demanding the right to exhibit in a separate hall near the Tuileries Palace. The participants included Odilon Redon, Seurat, Schuffenecker, Guillaumin, Dubois-Pillet, Henri-Edmond Cross and, in 1885, Angrand and Marie Bashkirtseff.

The exhibition presented the best examples of the new movement, which would eventually supplant the Impressionists. Some of the

Edgar DEGAS: *At the Milliner's.* Havemeyer Collection, The Metropolitan Museum of Art, New York. Precursor and companion of the Impressionists, Degas' universe encompassed all the aspects of urban life, including intimate representations of the universe of women.

Impressionist artists would even join the new movement, of which Félix Fénéon was the spokesman.

The Eighth Impressionist Exhibition of 1886 had the strange atmosphere of twilight in contrast to the dawn of a new generation of painters. It marked the end of an exemplary adventure and the emergence of a new movement, in which the role played by Pissarro would be determinate: that of a bridge between the Impressionists and the artists who were forging the new movement of Pointillism.

The Impressionist adventure had ended in conflicts and regrets. There were the participants of the first exhibition: Attendu, Brandon, Bureau, Colin, Desbras, Latouche, Meyer, de Molins, Mulot-Durivage, A. Ottin and Robert, who progressively fell into obscurity; Astruc, who had contributed so

Hugo BIRGER: *Artists Having Breakfast at the Café Ledoyen*. Göteborgs Konstmuseum, Göteborg.
Like Jean Béraud, Birger's keen eye and expressive brush captured precise instants in the social life of the period.

Mary CASSATT: *Young Woman at the Window*. The Corcoran Gallery of Art, Washington, DC.
The oft-repeated theme of posing a model before a window permitted the representation of two aspects of the environment, expressed here as a vista both man-made and natural.

Mary Cassatt

importantly to the movement; de Nittis, who the Goncourts so admired and who would make his way into the upper reaches of the official art establishment, navigating gracefully between the Salon and his Impressionist friends like Manet, who executed his first open-air painting, *Madame De Nittis et son fils Jacques (Mrs. De Nittis and Her Son Jacques)*, in his company; Degas who also painted Madame De Nittis, and Caillebotte, who used one of his

themes in his first works.

There were those who joined the group during the various exhibitions, such as Béliard, Cordey, Lamy, François, Lebourg, Legros, Lépine, Levert, Maureau, Piette, Vignon, Somm and Tillot; those who were naturally drawn into the movement for reasons of friendship or through intellectual and aesthetic sympathy, such as Bracquemond, Millet and Boudin; and the artists who after showing in most of the exhibitions,

Georges SEURAT: *Sunday at the Grande-Jatte*. Art Institute of Chicago. By its radically new techniques of representing reality, Seurat's monumental painting revolutionized the Impressionist movement. An entire generation of artists would adapt Seurat's pointillism, of which this work remains the most representative and spectacular example.

launched into new artistic directions which would undermine the very essence of the Impressionist aesthetic.

The Eighth Expressionist Exhibition revealed the supremacy of the theories of Seurat, who triumphed with *Un Dimanche à la Grande-Jatte (Sunday at the Grande-Jatte)*, followed by the acclaim accorded to Signac's *La Berge - Asnières (Riverbank at Asnières)*, *Les Gazomètres - Clichy (The Gasworks*

at Clichy) and *La Neige, boulevard de Clichy (Boulevard de Clichy Under the Snow)*. They testified to the growing force of a new aesthetic which Pissarro would employ in *Au jardin, mère et enfant (Mother and Child in the Garden)*, as would his son Lucien for the illustrations of one

Berthe MORISOT: *The Servant Girl.*
The National Gallery of Art, Washington, DC.
Berthe Morisot never established a hierarchy in her choice of subjects. For her, the most important criterion was the faithful representation of her immediate environment, including the most humble participants in her daily life.

of Octave Mirbeau's books.

A veritable coalition formed against Seurat. Guillaumin complained to Pissarro that Degas "had little or no knowledge of what Signac and Seurat were doing," and his doubts concerning the two painters. Berthe Morisot, who knew both of them well, attempted to reassure their critics, while Durand-Ruel's enthusiasm for their work provided added credibility. Pissarro would also declare that "Seurat contributed a new vision that the others, despite their talent, were not capable of appreciating, and that (he) was personally convinced that the advance represented by their art would one day produce extraordinary results."

Seurat, who was born in the 10th arrondissement of Paris in 1859, was a faithful resident of his neighborhood. Prior to entering the Fine Arts Academy, he had been a student at the public school on the rue des Petits-Hôtels. In 1882, he rented a studio at 16 rue de Chabrol. His *Baignade à Asnières (Bathing at Asnières)*, shown at the independent artists exhibition of 1884, was noticed by Fénéon, who became his most active defender. In 1885, he again took part in the independent artists' exhibition, presenting a preliminary study for *La Grande- Jatte* . The painting required a long and painstaking preparation consisting of twenty-seven panels, three canvasses and twenty-seven drawings. He worked in the same manner as film directors, thoroughly familiarizing himself with the site and even painting the background without any of the human figures which would ultimately occupy it. Each of the characters was sketched beforehand, and then fitted into the exact position it would occupy in the overall scene. By its calculated precision and quasi-scientific analysis of the relationships of colors, his method was at opposite ends from the spontaneous and emotional manner of the Impressionists.

Seurat was surrounded by painters faithful to the initial Impressionist principles, and whose fidelity suffered from the progressive disintegration of the movement.

Guillaumin *(Chaumière à Damiette - Cottage at Damiette)*, Mary Cassatt *(Jeune Fille à la fenêtre - Young Girl at the Window)*, Berthe Morisot *(Jardin à Bougival - Garden at Bougival)* and to a lesser degree Marie Bracquemond, all continued within the Impressionist current, while Degas *(Femme essayant un chapeau chez sa modiste - Woman Trying on a Hat)*, *(Suite de nus de femmes se baignant, se lavant, se séchant, s'essuyant, se peignant ou se faisant peigner - Women Bathing, etc.)* reaffirmed his original position, followed by his disciples J. L Forain *(Femme à sa toilette - Woman Bathing)* and Zandomeneghi.

Gauguin, who was preparing another sojourn at Pont-Aven, participated in the exhibition with works which included *Nature morte (Still Life)*, *Vache au repos (Resting Cow)* and *Un Coin de la mare (A Corner of the Pond)*. Schuffenecker, attracted by the Salon des Indépendants, discreetly exhibited alongside his friends Gauguin and Seurat. Henri Rouart, the gifted "amateur" painter, once again faithfully contributed his works (he had participated in all of the exhibitions except that of 1882), as did Tillot, who found himself in the ambiguous position of a painter involved in several other artistic endeavors. His style was representative of the transition between the Barbizon School and the generation which would define the Impressionist aesthetic. A journalist and friend of Degas, he was also a well-known collector of Japanese art and a familiar of literary and artistic circles of the period. Like Astruc, he helped contribute to the notoriety of the movement despite the negligible quality of his artistic production.

category which visibly had little to do with Impressionism. He had been invited by Guillaumin, whom he had previously encountered at the Salon des Indépendants and had criticized the Impressionists in his book *Dans le rêve (In the Dream)*, in which he energetically disclaimed any sympathy for the movement.

The incongruity of his presence in an Impressionist exhibition indicates

Vignon was also a member of the group of minor painters whose works appeared at the exhibitions to the detriment of the overall coherence of the movement's aesthetic principles.

Odilon Redon -*Tête laurée (Head with Laurels)*, *Le Secret (The Secret)*, *Homme primitif (Primitive Man)* and *Salomé* - was in a class by himself, a

Paul Signac: *Gas Tanks at Clichy*.
Felton Collection, The National Gallery of Victoria, Melbourne.
Even more than the Impressionists, the next generation of artists portrayed the new industrial landscapes that were transforming the outskirts of the large cities. Their vision was less an exaltation of natural beauty than the simple yet highly evocative representations of ordinary reality.

117

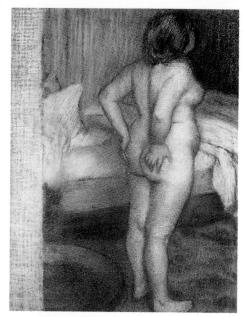

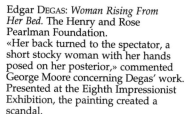

Edgar DEGAS: *Woman Rising From Her Bed*. The Henry and Rose Pearlman Foundation.
«Her back turned to the spectator, a short stocky woman with her hands posed on her posterior,» commented George Moore concerning Degas' work. Presented at the Eighth Impressionist Exhibition, the painting created a scandal.

the extent to which the movement's principles had become vague. The exhibition was less than that of a school of painting than a final attempt to federate a group of highly independent artists who had been rejected by the official institutions. Redon was already an accomplished artist and admired by Huysmans, who himself had abandoned naturalism for the seductive shores of symbolism.

His novel *A rebours (Other Way)*, which embodied the new aesthetic, would become the touchstone for the new movement. Following Octave Mirbeau's protest against his participation, Redon enlisted Mallarmé's support; his appearance at the tail-end of Impressionism was almost fortuitous.

The eighth exhibition signified the end of Impressionism as an organized movement. It coincided with the emergence of a new style whose principles and subjects were radically different from those of the preceding movement. The Impressionists, who celebrated the simple, everyday reality of a world whose idyllic nature was already disappearing under the onslaughts of technology, maintained the tradition of representing scenes of family life, motherly love, and a harmonious vision of existence.

This somewhat simplified world in which nature and humanity were still intact would collapse before the emergence of the Symbolist movement which abandoned reality for the universe of dreams and a mystical vision of man and the universe. In its refusal to represent the world as it was, it proposed another interpretation which was totally imaginary.

At the same time a new group of artists emerged, whose irreducible individualism placed them at the limits of what was considered aesthetically acceptable relative to the period. From Van Gogh to Gauguin, they became the martyrs of their own integrity as they developed a new current of art whose objective was to awaken the consciousness (and the conscience) of their fellow-men.

Edgar DEGAS: *Woman in a Tub*. Havemeyer Collection, The Metropolitan Museum of Art, New York.
Both art critics and the public attacked Degas for portraying the "overbearing shamelessness of the flabby and pitiful prostitute."

Edgar DEGAS: *Nude Drying Her Foot*. Orsay Museum, Paris.
In his series of intimate visions of women in their bath, Degas never attempted to falsify the reality of his models, depicting their bodies and gestures with brutal reality.

The Urban Landscape

Claude MONET: *The Infanta's Garden.*
Allen Memorial Art Museum,
Oberlin (OH).
The Impressionist painters often represented the public gardens of Paris. For
Monet, who also painted flower beds
and highly-landscaped pastoral scenes,
the representation of nature within an
urban context was both decorative and
symbolic.

*I*mpressionist Paris was a city
which had been entirely transformed
by Baron Haussmann's enormous
urban renewal project.

Abandoning its ancient heritage
of a walled city, Haussmann
dismantled its ramparts and
fortifications and constructed
generous promenades, majestic open
perspectives, and gracious buildings
whose homogenous style became the
hallmark of the period.

The influence of Napoleon the
Third was predominant. It was less a
style than an overall approach
influenced by his early impressions of
London and its rich network of parks
and gardens. This was combined
with a strategic policy of creating wide
boulevards permitting the movement
of government troops, for, at this
point in history, the real menace to
the state was considered to be the
people themselves rather than a
traditional invasion from the exterior.
This had become clear during the
French Revolution and confirmed
during the revolts of 1830 and 1848.
As the old quarters of the city were
gutted and demolished and replaced

by a rectilinear grid of streets,
boulevards and avenues, the political
establishment gained the absolute
mastery of demonstrations, crowd
control, and the possibility of quelling
popular revolts and insurrections. It
was a highly politicized form of
urbanization, based more on fear
than upon an idealized vision of the
potential of the city.

Haussmann's transformation was
most evident along the new avenues
and large boulevards that had
changed the physical aspect of the
city so radically as to actually modify
the behavior of its inhabitants.

The distinctive style of the
decorative arts which developed so
richly during the reign of Napoleon
the Third reflected the ostentatious
quest for luxury, authority and power
which constituted the very soul of
the period.

Impressionism also documented
life in the city during this period, from
the banks of the Seine (Renoir: *Le
Pont Neuf*, Monet: *Le Jardin de
l'Infante -The Infanta's Garden*) to the
wide new boulevards (Renoir: *Grands
boulevards*, Monet: *Le Boulevard des*

Capucines, Pissarro: *Boulevard extérieur)* as well as with the compelling aerial perspectives by Caillebotte.

To represent the multiplicity of the city with its movement and agitation upon the limited space of a canvas, painters framed their scenes as if they were photographs. The only difference was that photographers seized their subject in a static unchanging moment, whereas the Impressionist painters rendered the movement of the city through the very manner in which they painted. Rather than expressing the individual, their goal was to render palpable the city's movement as a collective phenomenon.

Pierre-Auguste RENOIR: *Grands Boulevards.* Philadelphia Museum of Art, Philadelphia.
Nearly all of the Impressionist painters, including those who chose to live and work in the country (such as Pissarro and Sisley), were also attracted by Parisian street scenes and the perspectives offered by Haussmann's renovation of the city. Their pictorial representations of Paris and its inhabitants were radically new and innovative.

Sidney STARR: *On the Imperial Coach*.
The National Gallery of Canada,
Massey Collection of English Painting,
Ottawa.
Fascinated by street scenes and their
crowds, Starr and many of the Impres-
sionists captured the perpetual move-
ment and excitement of the period.

Victor WESTERHOLM: *The Seine at Paris*. Turun Taidemuseo, Turkey. The strong interest of Scandinavian artists in the Impressionist movement resulted in an ongoing series of visits to Paris and the choice of similar themes as their French counterparts.

Armand GUILLAUMIN: *Sunset at Ivry*. Orsay Museum, Paris. Guillaumin was conscious of the more unpleasant aspects of urban life to a much higher degree than most of his fellow artists of the period. He represented the gradual transformation of the city in a series of paintings depicting the industrial suburbs of Paris.

Albert EDELFELT: *In the Luxembourg Gardens*. Ateneumin Taidemuseo, Helsinki. The atmosphere is agreeably luminous, the scene exudes the pleasures of being alive. A homage to the universe of the Countess of Ségur and Marcel Proust.

35 Boulevard des Capucines

*C*ertain addresses are like men: endowed with a strong personality and their own unmistakable character. Number 35 on the boulevard des Capucines was the address of Nadar's studio. Nadar was a central figure of his period. He was a photographer and journalist as well as a man of the world. All of the most brilliant people of Paris came to his studio to be photographed. His archives were like a hall of fame, filled with celebrities, reputations and glory.

His studio was a gathering-place for the young artists who united under the banner of the *Société des peintres, graveurs et sculpteurs,* the association which organized the First Impressionist Exhibition. By its location in the center of Paris, among theaters, fashionable cafés and shops, 35 boulevard des Capucines constituted a symbol; the paintings which were shown there were an outgrowth of the very atmosphere of the site itself.

If Impressionism represented a rediscovery of nature, it also profoundly expressed the city and its movement, lights and crowds. The rapid and fragmented brushwork of Impressionism was perfectly suited to the representation of the urban environment with its ceaseless movement and variety of themes. The new artistic vision of the

Impressionists was also perfectly adapted to the profound transformations of Paris by Haussmann's urban renewal program. A totally new city sprung up before their eyes, consisting of wide boulevards, green parks and opulent buildings. Paris was the playground of speculators, adventurers, dashing men and flirtatious women who inhabited a fantasy world straight out of the operettas of Offenbach. Established tradition and social barriers collapsed in the avid rush for pleasure; ambition and the desire for adventure knew no bounds, often among individuals who were the least prepared for this heady new liberty. Shaking the inertia of the middle classes, the Second Empire awakened the latent ambition among those determined to seize the moment and make their place in the new society that was emerging. It offered itself to every type of speculation and adventure; in its unrestrained dynamism it was the vision of the future.

Paris, whose historical center had been surgically removed and reconstructed like a huge theatrical set, was no longer the city described in Balzac's novels. The old physical and societal structures had been demolished forever and replaced by the brittle, noisy and dynamic capital portrayed by Zola: it was the city of

Claude MONET: *Boulevard des Capucines*. Pushkin Museum, Moscow.
The wide boulevards of the center of Paris were one of the essential theaters of social and cultural life in the latter half of the nineteenth century.

Nana and *Bel-Ami*. In a word, Paris had become modern.

Open to all the facets of the society of the period, Impressionism portrayed many of the features of the cynical and self-satisfied city.

Artists such as Degas and Manet, themselves products of the very classes which controlled and profited from this society, were particularly well-placed to comprehend and represent its rich psychological and physical characteristics. Their works provide an intimate vision of both the superficial and more profound aspects of Paris at the end of the nineteenth century.

The urban landscapes of Pissarro, Renoir, Monet and Caillebotte represented the environment with a light touch and frequent allusions to the charms of nature. It was often a

John Singer SARGENT: *In the Luxembourg Gardens*. Philadelphia Museum of Art; J.G. Johnson Collection, Philadelphia.
Sargent adapted the vivacious brushwork of Impressionism to the representation of elegant and formalized visions of the world of high society.

Paris of quiet gardens, wooded groves, and gracious parks. Nature was also represented in the artificial universe of greenhouses, where humans were portrayed like characters in a bourgeois comedy (*Dans la serre - In the Greenhouse* by Manet).

Other scenes were situated in the luxurious bourgeois dining rooms and salons similar to those frequented by Paul Bourget and Marcel Proust, whose constraining hypocritical atmosphere Maupassant portrayed in his short stories and novels.

Edouard MANET: *In the Greenhouse.* Staatliche Museen Preussischer Kultur-besitz, Berlin.
Artificially-preserved nature serves as the background for quiet conversations between cultivated and well-bred individuals.

A Long Peaceful River

*T*he history of painting is also the story of the places where it occurs and develops, for art always reflects the environment in which it is born. When dominated by the conventions of the Academy, painting was academic and conventional, representing scenes and landscapes as unsurprising as theatrical sets or the decors that used to appear in the backgrounds of ancient, stiffly-posed photographic portraits. The landscapes seemed to contain all known or imaginable landscapes, like an anthology of stories set in an eternally fictional dimension.

The current of naturalism would radically modify the principle through the representation of immediate reality. Impressionism would give it all of its force.

The history of Impressionism can be followed by simply looking at the map of the territory on which it developed.

Aside from the detours and voyages of the artists (Renoir on the Riviera, Monet in the Creuse, the retreat of Cézanne in Provence), the Impressionist movement rolled onward like a long, calm river.

Starting in Paris, the painters followed the Seine to the sea,

traversing a series of landscapes that unfolded from village to village. Their works reflected both their daily life and that of the period. The landscapes were not idealized (as was the case with Corot, who paradoxically was venerated by the Impressionists) but were exact and precise visual testimonials to moments in time, punctuated by the cycle of the four seasons.

They celebrated the pleasures of the riverside, chronicling the long and meandering course of the Seine through the lovely villages situated along its banks, where many of these same artists chose to live: Argenteuil, Bougival, Chatou, Louveciennes, and the magic circle of hamlets around Pontoise. Impressionist art and its artists continued the voyage to its ultimate limits - the estuary of the Seine, there where the great river pours out into the deeper waters of the Channel under a vast, luminous and ever-changing sky, the inspiration of canvases filled with the heady liberty of the sea and endless, open space.

Like Barbizon, Honfleur was one of the early geographical centers of Impressionism. This charming seaside fishing village on the coast of

Claude MONET: *The Beach at Sainte-Adresse*. Art Institute of Chicago. Monet's vision of the sea was the result of direct observation and early experiences. Like the Venus of mythology, Impressionism was born of the ocean.

Normandy attracted painters fascinated by the "marvelous clouds" evoked by Baudelaire, who was often a visitor. His description of Boudin's works was equally elegiac: "Those studies which so rapidly and faithfully rendered that which is so ephemeral and immaterial in form and color: waves and clouds. Fantastic and luminous, dark and chaotic, green or rose-colored immensity (...) affecting my mind like a heady beverage or like the eloquence of opium."

Baudelaire's poetic prose mirrored the objectives of the Impressionist manner itself, in which the artist merged with his subject and was impregnated by its essence. Ultimately, it was less an art of representation than the representation of pure, subjective sensation.

The sea, clouds and sky in their blue-green immensity inspired a new

Eugène BOUDIN: *On the Beach.*
Private Collection.
Boudin was one of the pioneers of Impressionism. He regularly painted beaches and seascapes as subjects worthy of being represented in their own right, an attitude which was at the opposite end of the canons of academic art of the period, characterized by the anecdote and historical reference.

form of painting which surged from the collective consciousness of artists like pure energy. Courbet would paint the beaches of Normandy, meditating on the sea and listening to its profound chant. Monet, following the wise advice of Boudin, who initiated him to open-air painting, would produce superb seascapes.

At the Ferme Saint-Siméon (like the Ganne Inn in Barbizon) painters gathered and exchanged their dreams and opinions. The difference of ages and generations was an element of vitality in a company of artists which included d'Isabey, Harpignies, Jongkind, Daubigny, Troyon, Amand Gautier, Diaz, Cals, Courbet, Boudin and Monet, who was the child of this gathering of talents drawn from so many horizons.

Their seascapes and beach scenes often represented the new vogue of sea-bathing (Boudin: *Sur la plage - On the Beach;* Monet: *Camille et sa cousine sur la plage de Trouville - Camille and Her Cousin on the Beach at Trouville;* Manet: *Sur la plage - On the Beach),* in works characterized by vivacious brushwork and generous light. Somewhere between Trouville and Cabourg, painting had entered the charmed and delicate universe which Proust would portray in his *Jeunes Filles en fleurs.*

Edouard MANET: *On the Beach.*
Orsay Museum, Paris.
The difference between Boudin's smooth manner and Manet's spontaneous and energetic brushwork is particularly clear here.

Claude MONET: *Sailboat Racing at Sainte-Adresse*. The Metropolitan Museum of Art, New York.
Open to the sky and the sea, the scene is essentially a hymn to the primal elements of nature.

William Merritt CHASE: *Exquisite Hours*. Amon Carter Museum, Fort Worth (TX).
A title in the form of a confession. The subject represents an instant in time, captured for eternity on Chase's canvas.

Berthe MORISOT: *In a Seaside Villa*. Norton Simon Foundation, Pasadena (CA).
In the latter-half of the nineteenth century the bourgeoisie discovered the pleasures of beaches and seaside resorts. Their visits and the rituals of their social life were documented by many of the best Impressionist artists.

The Moulin de la Galette

*A*lthough it exercised a strong attraction on visitors drawn to its semi-rural atmosphere, Montmartre was rarely inhabited by the Impressionists. One exception was Renoir, who successively lived at 18 rue Houdon, 37 rue Laval, 11 boulevard de Clichy, 33 rue La Rochefoucauld, 43 rue Caulaincourt and the Château des Brouillards. The collective existence of the Impressionists was concentrated below, at the limits of the boulevard, on the sloping rue des Martyrs, the rue Saint-Georges, Notre-Dame-de-Lorette, and the trajectories of friendship that conducted Degas from the rue Laval to the rue La Rochefoucauld to encounter his neighbor Gustave Moreau in a café or Cézanne in Père Tanguy's shop on the rue Clauzel.

Thus were reflected the precise itineraries in the works they inspired, while Renoir, solidly implanted in Montmartre, celebrated the charms of a landmark windmill that had been converted into a dance hall in his famous *Le Moulin de la Galette.*

It was located at 12 rue Cortot, adjacent to an ancient complex of buildings dating from the seventeenth century. The place resembled nothing so much as a farm, but with a panoramic view far over the rooftops of Paris. Here, standing tall, rose one of the last windmills of Montmartre, which once had boasted dozens. As the fields of wheat that once covered the hill progressively disappeared, it was decided to convert the buildings surrounding it into a dance hall and bar.

It was a simple, low-ceilinged edifice, with a small platform for the musicians and a circular gallery from

Pierre-Auguste RENOIR: *Le Bal du Moulin de la Galette*. Orsay Museum, Paris.
One of the most well-known Impressionist works, Renoir's painting is a brilliant mixture of joyousness, charm, sensuality and movement. In its depiction of the pleasures of ordinary men and women, it remains a touching evocation of a vanished epoch.

which the dancing couples could be observed. The dances were held on Sundays and holidays; the price of admission was twenty-five *centimes* for men, while women were admitted free. It was a place where people came in search of amusement and romantic encounters, animated by lively dance music and the flashing colors of the women's skirts. The clients were basically members of the lower classes, but the warmly sensual atmosphere was appreciated by several of the Impressionist painters such as Renoir or Degas, who lived nearby on rue Laval.

With its dance floor of beaten earth, illuminated by multicolored lanterns at night, the Moulin de la Galette was like a perpetual carnival. Whole families frequented it, and on Sunday afternoons the room was full of adults and young people from the neighborhood, napping children, and

Federico ZANDOMENEGHI: *Le Moulin de la Galette*. Private Collection.
The last of the great windmills of Montmartre attracted crowds of tourists as well as those who came for the amusements its cabaret and dance hall offered. The Moulin de la Galette rapidly became the distinctive symbol of "Gay Paris".

strutting would-be lovers on the look-out for feminine conquests.

Renoir appreciated its atmosphere of "liberty without the excesses of sordidness." After deciding to execute a painting of the interior and its habitual clients, he began searching for models. Jeanne, a young girl straight out of a novel by Maupassant (just sixteen years old, she would also be the model for *La Balançoire [The Swing]* painted in the garden of the rue Cortot), appears among her friends Franc-Lamy, Goeneutte, Lhote, Cordey, Gervex and Rivière.

Vincent VAN GOGH: *Le Moulin de la Galette*. Rijksmuseum Kröller-Müller, Otterlo.
During his short visits to Paris, Vincent encountered many of the Impressionists and often painted the same places that they portrayed in their own works.

The Perfume of Femmes Fatales

*T*hey were Zola's fictional *Nana* and her real-life counterparts. All were adored with ostentation; their perfumed bodies and immorality were their passport to success. The leading personalities of the Second Empire set the example by celebrating women whose beauty was surpassed only by their cynicism and calculating coldness. As playthings of the rich and powerful, their attraction often resided in their sulfurous reputations. Certain other men were drawn to them in reaction to the severe constraints imposed by their social station and class.

A mistress was also the symbol of personal success and the proof of one's own worth. Marriage, which often was only a thinly-disguised social arrangement in which any real pleasure or authentic eroticism was absent, drove those unable to play the hypocritical role which society had assigned them into the arms of illegitimate loves.

Zola, the pitiless observer of the mores of the period, offered the profile of the temptress whose charms were fatal for those who succumbed to them. In thrall to their own sterile egoism, these women sought the adoration of their admirers without giving anything of themselves: "One of Nana's pleasures was to undress in front of the mirror and contemplate herself from head to toe. Slipping out of her night-gown, she gazed at her nudity, forgetting all

else as the long moments passed. It was the pure passion for her own body, the delight in her own satiny skin and slender figure that rendered her so serious and attentive, totally absorbed in her love for herself."

Manet's painting of Nana represented the same theme of the mirror, as did Cézanne's *La Nouvelle Olympia*. Women were represented as desirable objects, as can be seen in Manet's *Olympia* .

Here the mirror and there the male *voyeur*. the fascination with their image operated strictly within the dimension of the visible, and within the mode of spectacle. The veritable existence of the femme fatale was anchored in the regard of those who contemplated her, even as she damned those men who saw in them the release from the mediocrity of their own existence.

As Armand Silvestre wrote in *Le Nu au Salon (The Nude in the Salon)*, "How often, seated at the terrace of a celebrated café on Avenue de Clichy that had been frequented by Zola, Manet, Duranty, Fantin-Latour, Degas and still other artists and writers, my friend Desboutin and I admired the beautiful girls passing by after finishing work on balmy summer evenings, often on the arm of their lovers, their eyes sparkling with happiness."

This was the image of femininity as seen by Renoir: a mixture of joyous sensuality and youthful freshness,

Edouard MANET: *Nana*. Hamburger Kunsthalle, Hamburg.
Nana, the prostitute of Zola's novel of the same name, was probably inspired by the real-life character of Valtesse de la Bigne, a celebrated courtesan of the period.

recalling the saucy seamstress or ribald peasant-girl. Like Gabrielle, the servant-girl whom the painter often used for the special manner in which light interacted on her skin, they were Renoir's usual type of models. Their femininity was no longer the dangerous, fatal variety of forbidden dreams, but something more familiar and reassuring, situated in everyday, normal and even joyous reality. They were the images of women barely out of childhood, captured during moments in the bath, dancing, or dressing themselves in the gay light-colored clothing they preferred. They innocently offered their youth and the freshness of their features; faces filled with light, in which the heaviness of psychological complexity was absent. Renoir's women were symbols of a femininity which found its expression

Paul CÉZANNE: *La Nouvelle Olympia*. Orsay Museum, Paris.
By this direct reference to Manet, the young Cézanne demonstrated his intention of forging a new manner of painting. His passionately baroque temperament has not yet been subdued and mastered.

Edouard MANET: *Olympia*. Orsay Museum, Paris.
A vision straight out of a poem by Baudelaire. Both the painter and the poet shared the opinion of women as the "fruit of sin". Here, Manet portrays Olympia as a shameless barbarian goddess.

in maternal love and daily acts of devotion.

At the other extreme of this reassuring yet dynamic vision of femininity was that of Degas, whose women were portrayed less in the exercise of their seductive powers than in their unvarnished intimacy.

Celebrated elsewhere in painting as idols of a cult of love, portrayed in a dimension of suspended time,

period's ideal of femininity, their existence was portrayed as the simple expression of their physical bodies.

Degas emphasized the commonness of these women, their lack of charm and their availability for romantic adventure - often the consequence of the position they occupied in society or a profession which left them vulnerable to the advances of masters, clients or the

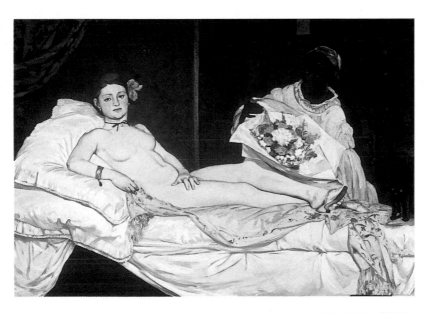

accompanied by symbols of devotion as if they were icons of religious art, Degas placed his women in the ruthless temporality of their bath. Their nudity was not a manifestation of innocence or original grace, but of necessity, in the cramped conditions of the small garret rooms habitually reserved for servants. These were the ablutions of the maid or seamstress, whose frank nudity reflected the casualness and vulgarity of their love-lives. Far from representing the

casual passer-by.

For other painters, if the image of the femme fatale was captured literally at sidewalk-level, it was because they often began and ended their careers there. Such was the case of 'La Goulue' (The Glutton), who became one of Toulouse-Lautrec's favorite models.

For the Impressionists, these women were less like those portrayed by the Symbolist painter Gustave Moreau - dripping with precious jewels (what Degas would call 'hardware'), than the type of woman who offered herself in a bordello with a shamelessness which excluded any sentimentality or illusion, placing her body within the context of a simple commercial transaction. Nana was just another woman for sale; her only true destiny was the ineluctable necessity of using her body as a means of escaping the misery of her material and social condition.

If the femme fatale had this ordinary, common quality for the Impressionists, the Symbolists represented her surrounded by an aura of mystery, placed in the decor of a palace or temple which signified both her innate distance and the inherent danger of approaching her. Impressionism did not project a mystical or disembodied vision of woman, but instead celebrated her ordinary qualities which encompassed the faithful companion, artistic muse or even venal prostitute, but without definitively enclosing her within any one of these (or the limitless number of other) identities, leaving her free to pass from one to the other as simple chance, destiny, or the vagaries of her spirit dictated.

Edgar DEGAS: *The Tub*. Orsay Museum, Paris.
Degas' constant fascination with the theme of women in the bath provoked contradictory reactions even from his staunchest supporters. Despite his underlying current of misogyny, Degas' manner of framing his subjects is remarkable and contains an implicit reference to the new art of photography.

Pierre-Auguste RENOIR: *Woman at
Her Bath*. Private Collection.
Even more than Degas, Renoir's vision
of women was voluptuous and
sensual.

Mallarmé, Intimately

Zola's approval of Manet's works corresponded to the element of social protest than ran through his own writings. As a young author, Zola's choice of the causes he would defend often corresponded to his desire to win recognition as a writer. His faithfulness to these causes could be somewhat relative, as seen by the publication of his novel *L'Œuvre* in 1886. This fictionalized account of the world of artists in late nineteenth-century Paris enlarged upon the already existing split among the Impressionists. For Zola, it was imperative that art be linked to social consciousness and commitment, and never a self-sufficient activity disconnected from the problems and conflicts of the real world.

Manet's relationship with Mallarmé was of a very different nature: infinitely more constant and productive.

When Mallarmé first encountered Manet, he was a young unknown poet newly arrived in Paris from his native village of Tournon, while Manet was already famous - especially for his liaison with the heady Nina de Callias. Their existence was thus already marked by the importance of women, who would continue to play the role of intermediary and muse throughout the careers of both men.

In his daily journey from the Lycée Condorcet to his apartment at 89 rue de Rome, Mallarmé would often stop off at Manet's residence on the rue de Saint-Petersbourg which, due to his reputation as an artist and the fact that he had become the target of every injustice of the period, had become one of the favorite gathering-places for the members of the Impressionist movement.

Manet's contacts with Mallarmé were particularly stimulating and productive of new works. As Henri Mondor noted, each artist, "the offspring of an ancient line of city-dwellers," was attracted by the energy of the other, adding that "each perceived the deep, authentic and innovative qualities found in the other's work."

When Mallarmé defended his friend in the article entitled *The Jury for Painting of 1874 and Manet,* his

Edouard MANET: *Resting Woman*.
Museum of Art, Rhode Island School
of Design, Providence (RI).
Berthe Morisot, Manet's sister-in-law
and frequent model is here portrayed
in a moment of liberty and tender
complicity. It is interesting to compare
the work with Monet's *Portrait of
Mallarmé*.

prose was forthright and clear even though his poetry had progressively become more abstract in that quest for the purity of expression which would one day be mirrored by painting.

Lucid to the point of being totally convincing, he stated: "What is meant by saying a work does not go far enough when all of its elements are cohesive and its fragile charm can be so easily destroyed by an additional touch?"

The brotherly spirit of complicity between the two artists resulted in the publication of one of the first collaborations between an artist and a poet: Edgar Allen Poe's *The Raven*, translated by Mallarmé and illustrated with five striking drawings by Manet. Mallarmé had realized Baudelaire's long-standing desire to translate Poe's haunting and enigmatic work. *The Raven* was followed by a new project and joint-collaboration between the two artists, *The Afternoon of a Faun*. The edition consisted of a thin volume graced by a series of Manet's drawings. Catulle Mendès, who received a copy, described it thusly: "two thin silk cords, one black and the other pink, traverse the covers and join in a fragile button at the bottom, providing an air of frivolous mystery to the gray Japanese cardboard envelope whose tones are sunny, silky, soft and resistant at the same time, as fleshy as if made from the pulp of a tiger lily, and upon which the ancient title is embossed in golden letters.... And the poem? It would be easier to describe the song of the nightingale... It is not obscure, but strange, subtle, prolonged, tormented, new, rare and luminous...".

Manet's participation recalled an unrealized project for the illustration of Zola's *Contes à Ninon (Ninon's Stories)* that dated from 1866, which had finally been concretized in *The Cats* by Champfleury in 1868, an additional collaboration with Banville for "The Polichinelle" in 1874 and with Charles Cros for *The River*.

Manet's high degree of intellectual complicity resulted in a portrait whose technique was radically different than that of Zola, emphasizing the rupture of painting with its own past and signifying an innovation of impressions and the use of brush-stroke and line. Even more than Gauguin or Whistler, the image of Mallarmé that appeared in a volume of his poems was an authentic and subtle reflection of his private life.

In Manet's portrait, Mallarmé appears lying on a sofa surrounded by a decor of Japanese fabrics (which also appear in the portrait of Nina de Callias). It is a portrait of the poet who would be adulated by successive generations of writers and artists during his famous Tuesday afternoon salons on the rue de Rome. Like Manet's studio, Mallarmé's modest apartment became the gathering-place for the most brilliant spirits of the time. The entire intellectual and artistic elite of Paris would pass through its doors in an immense and ongoing gathering of kindred spirits. It was a privileged place of good will and friendship, and quite unlike the gossipy and back-biting atmosphere of 'The Grenier', the Goncourts' meeting-place in Auteuil, which was practically a club for misogynists.

Visitors to Mallarmé's apartment came for a ritual of the purest, most ethereal and timeless poetry. The influence of Manet and Impressionism upon Mallarmé was so great that, after Manet's death,

Mallarmé developed his style of writing beyond the established limits of the period, and ultimately became the virtual godfather of Symbolism.

His manner was announced by Manet, who employed the same dreamlike yet powerful nonchalance in his portrayal of Berthe Morisot in *Le Repos (Rest)*.

René Ghil, for whom Mallarmé wrote the preface for his collection of poetry, described him exactly like Manet's portrait: "Of ordinary stature, his portrait the air of an icon: that of an era of absolutes, of which Rimbaud, Lautréamont and he would be the heroes, accompanying the Impressionists in their irrepressible quest of modernity through a new and inviolate artistic expression.

he was lean rather than thin and possessed a natural grace and measure in the movements of his body. Nothing about him was heavy. His face reflected an intense spirituality and calm elegance."

As the emblematic symbol of all that art and poetry signified at the end of the nineteenth century, Mallarmé's fine, dreamy features give

Edouard MANET: *Woman with Fans*. Orsay Museum, Paris.
Gifted with an extraordinary understanding of female psychology, Manet expressed all of his model's fascination and voluptuousness in his portraits. His approach was the antithesis of that of Berthe Morisot.

The Gardens of Giverny

Claude MONET: *Flower Garden.*
Orsay Museum, Paris.
The most humble corner of a garden was sufficient to inspire Monet's genius for expressing a colorful riot of plants and flowers.

*A*fter years of wandering from place to place, Monet (like Renoir) finally became somewhat more sedentary. In 1883, he rented a large and comfortable house in Giverny and installed his wife and children. Family life was joyous in the spacious house and its surrounding gardens and orchards. The house itself was a long, one-story construction flanked by two low, slate-roofed barns painted a tender pink. There was also a lovely view over the vast garden: "in the foreground, two large black yew trees framed a path lined by spruces and box trees. On the right and to the west, a stand of lime trees screened a small building facing the main gate and the street that led to the village. To the south, the orchard was in blossom. Below it, a path and a railway line on an embankment. Beyond the embankment, a stream (the Ru), bordered by willows, poplars and flat fields. Far in the distance, a vague line of hills marked the left bank of the Seine. The sparkling spring light of the Ile-de-France made the colors sing."

It was here that Monet would discover his floral palette; but his greatest concern seemed to be diverting water from the Epte River for the lily pond which would become one of his favorite subjects.

Claude MONET: *Jeanne Marguerite Lecadre in a Garden*. Museum of the Hermitage, Saint-Petersburg.
The essence of women and flowers were expressed with perfect equanimity, as if both embodied the same vision of the beauty of existence.

His taste for a sedentary existence was an astonishing transformation for this inveterate wanderer, who would nevertheless still take working holidays on the French Riviera, at Etretat; in Holland; on Belle-Ile, in the Creuse at the poet Maurice Rollinat's house; in Norway, London and Venice; and in Rouen to paint the Cathedral.

Having finally acquired the house at Giverny in 1890, he began to enlarge his property parcel by parcel of land, like a peasant increasing his holdings. For Monet, it was less a reflex of a land-owner than that of an artist creating the ultimate in outdoor studios. He insistently and tirelessly painted the theme of nature and flowers, richly and subtly

Claude MONET: *Boat at Giverny*. Orsay Museum, Paris.
The beautiful landscaping of Monet's property in Giverny was captured in scenes portraying his family in the idyllic decor of his pastoral paradise.

organized to the point that the gardener's art merged with that of the painter. Monet established a place to practice his art in an environment which nourished it so exclusively that his approach became nearly Oriental in its radical integration within his own personality.

Impressionism, which began as a festive, nomadic art practiced by itinerants (of the city as well as the countryside) would, between Cézanne's images of the Montagne Sainte-Victoire and Monet's water lilies, realize its objectives and open painting to new forms of expression until ultimately exhausting its creative possibilities.

As it approached its outer boundaries, the genius of these two

Lilla Cabot PERRY: *Landscape at Giverny: Monet's Garden*. Private Collection.
Perry's admiration for Monet resulted in his purchase of a house in Giverny. Equally influenced by Pissarro, her approach to Impressionism was marked by a subdued, subtle manner.

artists became apparent. Cézanne's bitter and heady solitude was that of the ascetic, transforming the burning luminosity of the Midi until it revealed its inherent intensity of the void; Monet, like a patriarch in the middle of his family, hosting the Sunday lunches which were also touching reunions of old friends, for Giverny had also become a place of pilgrimage.

In time, the surroundings would become the site of an artists' colony populated chiefly by Americans, who particularly appreciated the Impressionist art that had been so energetically promoted by Durand-Ruel and which had enchanted a cultural environment still touched by primitivism. From 1890 until Monet's death in 1926, Giverny was the scene of family life and warm

Gustave CAILLEBOTTE: *The Gardener*.
Private Collection.
Like Monet in Giverny, Caillebotte preferred the calm environment of Yerres and Gennevilliers. His paintings of gardens reflected his appreciation for the charms of peaceful rural life.

encounters, where painting followed
the cycle of the seasons in a continual
and marvelous celebration of nature's
endless renewal.

William Merritt CHASE: *The Nursery*.
Richard Manoogian Collection.
Chase was one of the most enthusiastic
disciples of Impressionism in the
United States. His style was marked
by distinction and subtlety.

The Charmed Circle

Gustave CAILLEBOTTE: *Interior Scene with Woman at the Window*. Private Collection.
Although he painted intimate scenes of bourgeois life, Caillebotte's attitude was never complacent. His works often communicated a discreet but effective message of personal and social tensions and, as here, the unspoken conflicts between husbands and wives.

*F*or the decorative arts, the Second Empire was an extremely rich and prolific period. The acquisitiveness of the bourgeoisie, following the example of the Empire and imitating its pronounced taste for splendor, would stimulate the production of luxurious articles destined for the upper middle-classes.

The works of the Impressionist painters mirrored the image of a comfortably bourgeois and generally traditional existence: Manet's house-plants and the overheated hothouse atmosphere of velvet-draped private boxes at the theater; the opulence of the bouquets of Degas; the Sunday tables with their clutter of finished meals (Manet) or the rituals of calm interiors (Caillebotte, Monet); rag-pickers, hairdressers, prostitutes (Manet); and an ongoing series of light-hearted portraits (Berthe Morisot). The Impressionists portrayed the lyricism of daily life, calm existences devoid of drama and excitement, where the concept of the heroic had been replaced by images of the reassuring and familiar, often that of friend, companion or beloved in the tranquil complicity of a soft and comforting universe.

If Degas occasionally gave expression to scenes filled with silent tragedy, the context was less that of daily reality than that of an intimate, personal dimension of his own imagination, or as in *Le Viol (The Rape)*, inspired by the blackest and most cynical pages of naturalist literature.

It was an existence of acquired privileges and comfort, whereas the preceding generation had entered life as if in a raging storm. Society profited from its gains, the relative peace and a level of comfort propitious to the expression of a certain sensuality. The facade of bourgeois and hypocritical respectability would eventually disintegrate under the repeated attacks of a dissident vision of reality, but these future storms were for the moment absent from the calm horizon of Impressionism.

From Zola's 'Nana' to 'Aunt Bertha' (Morisot), the tonality was the same; only the contexts changed. Women were represented in all their

Paradoxically, Impressionism which celebrated the movement of fleecy clouds, the ephemeral quality of light, the flow of rivers, the charm of fresh-fallen snow and the glorious rebirth of nature in spring, would also subtly represent a gallery of more ambiguous characters whose existential doubts and conflicting emotions were so lucidly qualified by Stefan Zweig as "the confusion of sentiments."

variety, from the seductresses in their bedrooms (Manet's Nina de Callias) to the actresses who would declaim the acid lines of Labiche or Feydeau, denouncing the hypocritical mores of an exhausted society, and including Monet's representations of Camille or Berthe Morisot by Manet, reigning over an interior universe where all drama was smothered under the wall hangings and heavy period furniture.

Mary CASSATT: *Tea Time*. Museum of Fine Arts, Boston.
An understated affirmation of the somewhat selfish comfort of a way of life cultivated by a class which had insulated itself from the more unpleasant aspects of reality.

The Bar of the Folies-Bergère

Pierre-Auguste RENOIR: *The Private Box*. Courtauld Institute Galleries, London.

The world of theater and music halls exercised a fascination upon Renoir, who portrayed much of their ordinary but often ephemeral beauty. Here, by emphasizing the vibrant charm and desirability of the woman rather than (or despite) her social station, Renoir has transgressed the unspoken rules governing class attitudes during this period.

*F*or Huysmans, the Folies-Bergère was "the only place in Paris which stank so wondrously of love for hire and the stale lassitude of corruption." Baudelaire, a contemporary, penned another description, even more Impressionist in its style: "Illuminated by the soft luminosity of the theater-lights, receiving and reflecting it in their eyes, jewels and the whiteness of their shoulders, the young women appear as resplendent as portraits, framed in their private boxes. Members of the best families, some are grave and serious while others are blond, ethereal and gay. Some reveal the outlines of their precocious busts or adolescent cleavage with aristocratic casualness. With their expressions masked by their fans and their eyes sweeping across the hall or focused on a detail, they are as theatrical and striking as the opera or play that they are pretending to watch."

Numerous artists (Renoir, Degas, Mary Cassatt, Manet) would chose to represent the universe of the theater and music halls, with their social rituals, splendid clothing, vanity and atmosphere of luxury.

From legitimate theater to the often ribald entertainment of music halls, the distance is short. It was

repeatedly traversed by a certain type of client whose wealth, social position and education provided the self-confidence, exquisite politeness and poise needed for moving with ease from one universe to the other. More than any other artist of the period, Manet typified this type of wandering spectator. As was customary with a gentleman of his station, he frequented the universe of the theater; it was part of his daily life, a self-contained environment complete with friends and established rituals and habits. The stage was a perfect focal-point for his imagination and fantasies, a place where he graphically expressed his conception of women in general, and in particular in his *Un Bar aux Folies-Bergère*.

There, he might have encountered Guy de Maupassant, who described it so well in *Bel-Ami* as the perfect setting for an unexpected adventure with a beautiful stranger, a ritual of initiation into the softer secrets of Parisian life: "Like a fine mist, a cloud of tobacco smoke masked the stage from the far side of the hall. The smoke of the cigars and cigarettes clung like white mist to the ceiling, accumulating under the large dome, around the chandelier and above the balcony and its spectators. In the vast corridor that leads to the circular promenade filled with bejeweled women and the darker masses of men, a separate group of females waits for customers in front of three counters behind which can be seen three heavily made-up and tired-looking women selling drinks and love, as tall mirrors reflect their backs and the faces of the passers-by."

In his novel *Le Ventre de Paris (The Belly of Paris)*, Zola would evoke both the bar and its "beautiful Lisa, who leaning against the counter (...) on that particular day, was superbly fresh: the whiteness of her apron and sleeves matched that of her shoulders and fat neck, above which her pink cheeks glowed like rosy hams marbled with transparent grease."

Despite the somewhat more populist description offered by Zola, the register remains extremely close to that chosen by Manet. For both artists, it was a scene which was more artificial than authentically sensual, in which the image of women was the reflection of the larger spectacle of society, their distant and icon-like quality touched by the melancholy of places meant for the amusement of the masses.

Mary CASSATT: *Woman in a Private Box*. Charlotte Dorrance Wright Collection, Philadelphia Museum of Art, Philadelphia.
In the nineteenth century, the private box was as an important part of theater-going as the spectacle itself. Fascinated by the importance or beauty of the personalities seated within them, the eyes of the audience were often as riveted on the occupants of private boxes as upon the stage.

Edgar DEGAS: *Curtain Call*. Orsay
Museum, Paris.
Theater-going, opera and ballet
punctuated much of Parisian social life
during the late nineteenth century.
Actresses and dancers populated the
erotic imagination of a society which
although superficially respectable, in
reality practiced a double and often
totally hypocritical standard of
morality.

The Grande-Jatte

A long, narrow island in the middle of the Seine, just outside the city limits of Paris, the Grande-Jatte was where the common people of Paris went for relaxation and amusement. It served as a subject for many of the Impressionists, from Manet to Degas, as well as for the pointillist painter, Seurat.

Imperceptibly, the noble and historic capital was being transformed into a modern city, complete with its industrial suburbs inhabited by the new urban proletariat. Impressionist painting documented the transition from the bourgeois universe of pleasure, luxury, order and comfort to the raw world of the working poor. Manet, the son of an upper middle-class family, remained within the boundaries of his rank and station. On the occasions when he explored other social universes, fascinated by the strangeness of their atmosphere and inhabitants, it was within the ambiguous context of the theater. Seurat would penetrate even farther within the existence of the common people and the expression of his own vision of their world.

Paris was a vast territory whose contours were being explored by Impressionist artists who exalted its singularities and celebrated its newness. It was practically the first time that artists represented the common people and their haunts. Up until then, painting had been an activity practiced by responsible, serious individuals often close to if not directly participating in the official artistic and political structures of the period. By personal loyalty and natural allegiance, their art served society by reflecting its conventions and beliefs, often through mythological themes whose allegorical symbolism tended to justify the established power-structure.

Impressionism often explored the more futile, less serious aspects of existence. Following the example of the period poets who frequented the "lower depths" of Paris, haunting its ill-famed pleasure-spots, painters set up their easels in tinseled dance-halls and cabarets, capturing their over-heated, festive and ephemeral atmosphere.

At the same time, Paris offered numerous calm and picturesque subjects in the semi-rural zones that stretched beyond its city limits, far from the bar of the Folies-Bergère and its distinguished elderly gentlemen discretely observing the young women of questionable morals offering their bodies to the highest bidder. There was also the Paris of empty lots and industrial wastelands that Seurat would haunt, capturing here the stark silhouette of a factory and there the bleak public baths, to finish in the apotheosis of the Sunday ritual of the Grande Jatte, the triumph of the common man and his conquest of leisure.

The atmosphere had something of the circus parade that he loved so much: the animated, colorful spectacle of the people at play. It was a veritable fresco of the common man, from the modest couple in their best Sunday dress to the local

Complementary, but executed in a manner so radically different as to illustrate the evolution of painting during this period, only two years separates them. But already, Seurat's approach suggests a totally different vision of the world. The transformation is less in the class of people represented than in the manner in which the painter expresses their essence.

youngsters, reclining momentarily on the banks of the Seine before moving on to new adventures and encounters. If the *Bar of the Folies-Bergère* is a snapshot of Parisian populism, the *Island of the Grande-Jatte* is the reflection of the life in working-class suburbs. The two paintings (both major works of the period) echo and complement each other like two pages of the same story.

Georges SEURAT: *L'Ile de la Grande-Jatte*. Whitney Collection, New York. The final work was preceded by numerous sketches and preliminary versions. Seurat prepared his canvas like a director establishing the scenes of his film, including on-site visits to familiarize himself with the place.

International Currents

*T*he circulation of artistic currents across Europe was an extremely ancient phenomenon. Each country claimed to be the birthplace of a particular movement or style. For France, this was Impressionism.

The international reputation of Paris as a center of the arts attracted painters from all over the world. As they set up their easels on the same sites as those frequented by the Impressionists, they expressed the same freshness and spontaneity as their French counterparts. And after returning to their home-countries, they continued painting in the same manner.

Both in France and in Europe (as well as to a certain extent in the United States), art expressed an image of the lifestyle which would continue until the cultural shock produced by the First World War, which would definitively mark the end of Impressionism's generous and discretely positive vision of reality.

The essential characteristics of Impressionism remained constant, despite the variety of political and social systems of the countries which participated in the collective adventure of the movement. When modified, it was by forces which were external and often opposed to its basic nature, and in particular, local particularities and the tangible effects of the burgeoning industrial society. Impressionism was generally in a position of opposition if not outright rebellion in relation to the omnipresent power of the official art establishment. It was a movement touched by the spirit of adventure and the desire for independence, reflecting similar transformations which were affecting literature and specifically poetry and whose roots were found in the small group of French artists such as Renoir, Monet, Sisley, Pissarro, Caillebotte and Degas, who imposed a new manner of expressing visual reality.

In Germany, shaken by the difficult and chaotic unification of its principalities, Impressionism was represented by three excellent artists: Max Liebermann (1874-1935), Lovis Corinth (1858-1925) and Max Slevogt (1868-1932).

In Austria and Hungary, European powers of the first magnitude at the end of the nineteenth century, music predominated over painting. But

even if art lacked much of the official impetus found elsewhere, it was nevertheless heavily influenced by the bourgeois conventions of the period. A variety of tendencies influenced these painters, for other than Paris or Barbizon, there was also Munich - itself a center of the arts during this time - and the Worpswede School, a veritable hive of young talent and residence of the poet Rilke. The major figures of this hybrid generation were Karoly Ferenezy (1862-1917) and Lazlo Paal (1846-1879), whose works reflected the stylistic current of the Barbizon School.

Hanna PAULI: *Breakfast*. National Gallery, Stockholm.
All of the ingredients of a certain idea of happiness are united in this vision of an ordinary moment of daily life. The atmosphere of untroubled serenity is almost palpable.

Henry Herbert LA THANGUE: The
Orchard. City Art Gallery and
Museum, Cartwright Hall, Bradford.
A highly civilized approach to the
portrayal of nature, here used as a
backdrop in the representation of the
two women. A reassuring, bourgeois
yet realistic vision of a quiet afternoon
in the country.

The Scandinavian countries were
generally open to stylistic innovations
which reinforced and accelerated
their own movement away from the
conventions of the studio in favor of a
more naturalistic representation of
nature, traditionally one of their
favorite subjects. The Danish painters
Theodor Philipsen (1840-1920) and
Pedor Kroyer (1851-1909) had direct
contacts with Paris; Gauguin's wife
Mette was Danish, as was Viggo

Johansen (1851-1935). Norwegian artists such as Harriet Backer (1845-1932) were heavily influenced by their French counterparts, and particularly Fritz Thaulow, Gauguin's brother-in-law, whose work was characterized by an exceptional sense of form and atmosphere. The same held true for the even more diversified artistic and literary output of Christian Krogh (1852-1925). Sweden also participated in the movement, notably through several major artists such as Carl Hill (1849-1911), who had close ties with the Paris Impressionists, and Ernst Josephson (1851-1906). The latter, in addition to being a writer much admired by August Strindberg, was also a painter who contributed to the transformation of Swedish art through the introduction of the subjective element of feeling.

The Impressionist current influenced artists as far away as Russia, where it resulted in works of rare quality. Ilia Répine (1844-1871), Isaac Lévitan (1860-1900) and Valentin Serov (1865-1911) were among its most important adepts, their paintings characterized by a vision of vast horizons marked by the cadence of the seasons. Although the social and philosophical dimension of Russian art was more pronounced than in any other country at the time, it was never intrusive to the point of masking the tradition of naturalism prevalent among these artists.

At the cross-roads of Europe and the movement of the diversity of its artistic currents, painting in Switzerland reflected a diversity of non-national influences and a tradition of great collections, all of which stimulated the ongoing transformation of local production. Ferdinand Hodler (1853-1918) was one of the key figures of Swiss

Impressionism, a movement rich in minor artists such as Auguste de Molins and Léon-Paul Robert, both of whom were included in the First Impressionist Exhibition of 1874 in Paris. Hodler's manner went beyond the strict limits of the movement: he would traverse it guided by a vision which he shaped to his own ends. While his work reflected certain analogies and similarities of technique, it was Impressionist in the

Ilia RÉPINE: *Tolstoy Reading in a Forest.* Tretiakov National Gallery, Moscow. One of the most famous Russian painters of the period evoking one of the nation's most celebrated writers in a simple and natural context. It is instructive to compare Répine's painting of Tolstoy to Manet's *Portrait of Mallarmé*: here, the evident identification with the peasant-class, there, the exquisite subtlety of Manet's elitist vision.

sense that, situated within the context of the latter half of the nineteenth century, the movement embodied all new tendencies of artistic expression.

This diversity is particularly clear in the case of England, which provided Impressionism with two of its principal forerunners (Constable and Turner) and remained in constant interaction with the French movement, particularly during the London exile of certain members of the group during the Franco-Prussian war of 1870. To the urbane and literary exchanges which developed around major British art figures such as Whistler, others such as Sargent and Sikert added the touch of worldliness so exquisitely practiced by the Impressionists. (Manet, their master in all, expressed it best.) They forged key links between the Impressionism of the fields (born at the Barbizon school) and the Impressionism of the cities (Degas, Caillebotte, Manet). Their literary echo was Proust, whose writings both reflected and were nourished by the discoveries and often subversive resonance of the Impressionists themselves. At the opposite end of the thoroughly elitist approach of artists such as Whistler was the Impressionist current exemplified by the group of English artists which included Sir George Clausen (1852-1944) and Henry Herbert la Thangue (1859-1929). The movement was increasingly popular while largely going beyond the chronological limits of the history of Impressionism. Decidedly more populist, both through their approach and in their treatment of urban and rural landscapes in the manner of the French Impressionists, painters such as Sydney Starr (1857-1925) and above all Philip Wison Steer (1860-1942) were close to the vivacious and luminous brushwork of the Argenteuil period.

Impressionism in the United States was heavily influenced by the example of the French masters, introduced through the intermediary of Mary Cassatt (who initiated the marvelous Havemeyer collection) and the promotional efforts of Durand-Ruel. The dynamism of the American artists, characterized by a synthesis between the established tenets of academic painting and the new luminosity of Impressionism, was particularly apparent in the works of John Singer Sargent (1856-1925), who alternated distinguished portraits with compositions stylistically close to those of Monet. Childe Hassam (1859-1935), whose poetic vision of the city was similar to that of Caillebotte, was heavily influenced by his French Impressionist counterparts, as was William Merrit Chase (1849-1916). The enthusiasm for the movement resulted in the creation of a group of young American artists in France, many of whom settled in and around Giverny in the wake of Monet, and whose principal members included Theodor Robinson (1852-1896), Louis Ritter (1854-1892), John Leslie Breck (1860-1892), and the Canadian William Blair Bruce (1859-1906).

The international attraction of Impressionism was such that veritable

Federico de MADRAZO: *The Fortuny Gardens*. Prado Museum, Madrid. The painting is the result of the collaboration between Mariano Fortuny and the artist, who had married his daughter. The work marked the beginning of the recognition of nature as a subject in itself and is a forerunner of the Spanish current of Impressionism with its characteristically vivacious colors.

artists' colonies sprang up in other regions of France as well, notably in the village of Grez-sur-Loing. Situated on the edge of the Fontainebleau Forest, it drew artists from diverse horizons and nationalities, all of whom would contribute to the Impressionist adventure: the Americans Birge Harrisson, William Glackens (1870-1938) and Ernest Lawson (1873-1939); the Scandinavians Carl Larsson (1853-1919), Johann Rosen (1843-1923) and Bruno Liljefors (1860-1939); and the Canadian James Wilson Morrice (1865-1924). The presence of Sisley, who lived in the village of Moret in the immediate vicinity, contributed to the ongoing attraction of the region for artists from all over the world.

Although Dutch painting never made enormous inroads in France, its traditions influenced many artists working outside of its frontiers, such as Jongkind, while the rich heritage of the Hague School inspired the specific realism of artists such as Van Gogh.

Impressionism was particularly well-received in Belgium, where there were strong and reciprocal cultural exchanges with France. More liberal in spirit, the country was a haven for artists who had failed to receive critical acclaim in France. Their success in Belgium was principally due to the enthusiasm of a small group of dynamic connoisseurs who introduced and promoted their works in unofficial exhibitions. In stylistic terms, the Tervueren School in the Brabant was an equivalent of Barbizon. But the development of the Belgian school was particularly apparent in the neo-Impressionist movement, fostered through the efforts of poets such as Emile Verhaeren.

Spanish painting had enjoyed an excellent reputation in France since the era of Louis-Philippe. It had been promoted by the romantics and defended by writers such as Théophile Gautier. It was also highly important for Manet, and through his influence, an entire generation of French artists. One of the most characteristic Spanish Impressionists was Dario de Regoyos Valdès (1857-1913), while the Catalonian current was embodied in the work of Eliseo Meifren y Roig (1859-1940) and Francisco Gimeno Arasa 1860-1932).

Anna ANCHER: *Sunlight in the Blue Room*. Skagens Museum, Skagen. Ancher painted with Kröyer, Krogh and the artists of Skagen (the Scandinavian equivalent of Barbizon), her birthplace.

Similar to that of England, the role of Italy was particularly complex. The Macchiaioli movement was profoundly similar to French Impressionism and produced artists such as Telemaco Signorini (1835-1901), Giovanni Fattori (1825-1908) and Silvestro Lega (1826-1895), while others, like Zandomeneghi and De Nittis, were directly involved in the development of the French movement.

Alexandre Valentin SÉROV: *Young Girl with Peaches*. Tretiakov National Gallery, Moscow.
A celebrated portraitist, Sérov captured the essence of his subjects as precisely as a photographer, endowing his works with their particularly evocative quality.

Artists and Biographies

The Major Impressionists

BAZILLE Frédéric (1841-1870)
CAILLEBOTTE Gustave (1848-1894)
CASSATT Mary (1845-1926)
CÉZANNE Paul (1839-1906)
DEGAS Edgar (1834-1917)
FANTIN-LATOUR Henri (1836-1904)
GUILLAUMIN Armand (1841-1927)

MANET Edouard (1832-1883)
MONET Claude (1840-1926)
MORISOT Berthe (1841-1895)
PISSARRO Camille (1830-1903)
RENOIR Auguste (1841-1919)
SISLEY Alfred (1839-1899)

Secondary and Minor Impressionists

ATTENDU Antoine. Participated in the First Impressionist Exhibition with four still-lifes and two anecdotal subjects.

BÉLIARD Edmond-Joseph (1832-1912). Exhibited in the first and second Impressionist exhibitions. A regular client of the Café Guerbois and a friend of Manet, Zola, Guillaumin and Pissarro. After a promising start, heralded by Paul Alexis, he limited his production to peaceful landscapes of Ile-de- France (Pontoise, L'Isle-Adam and Etampes, the village in which he died).

BRANDON Edouard (1831-1897). An art collector and a friend of Degas, he participated in the First Impressionist Exhibition.

BUREAU Pierre Isidore (1827-1880). A friend of Ribot and Boudin, he exhibited at the Salon and participated in the exhibition of the *Refusés*. Briefly associated with the Impressionists, he took part in their first and second exhibitions.

COLIN Gustave. (1828-1911). A forerunner of Impressionism, admired by Monet and Pissarro. After a fortuitous participation in the First Impressionist Exhibition, he returned to the official Salons, where his works were well-received.

CORDEY Frédéric (1854-1911). A close friend of Renoir (who portrayed him in *L'Atelier de la rue Saint-Georges* and *Le Bal du Moulin de la Galette*), he was included in the Third Impressionist Exhibition. He lived in the vicinity of Pontoise, which served for many of his subjects. Painted in a manner similar to that of Pissarro.

DEBRAS Louis (1819-1899). After regularly exposing at the Salons, Debras participated in the First Impressionist Exhibition - his first and last experience with the group.

FRANÇOIS Jacques. The pseudonym of a female painter who participated in the Second and Third Impressionist Exhibitions.

LAMI Eugène (1800-1890). A painter and engraver appreciated for his equestrian subjects, Lami exhibited at the Luxembourg Museum.

LATOUCHE Louis (1829-1884). Exhibited at the First Impressionist Exhibition and thereafter at the official Salons. He was also an art supplies merchant and art dealer, with a shop on the corner of rue Laffitte and rue La Fayette. He collected works by his painter friends, such as Monet.

LEVERT Jean-Baptiste Léopold. Exhibited his paintings of landscapes of Ile-de-France (Essonne, Malesherbes, Fontainebleau, Barbizon) at the First, Second, Third and Fifth Impressionist Exhibitions.

MAUREAU Alphonse. The friend of Manet, Desboutin and Degas. A member of the circle of Nina de Callias, he participated in the Third Impressionist Exhibition.

MEYER Alfred (1832-1904). A specialist of oven-fired porcelain glazes, Meyer worked for the Manufacture de Sèvres and published a book on the technique. Meyer showed his work at the Salon as well as the First Impressionist Exhibition. His paintings were extremely conventional representations of historical subjects.

MOLINS Auguste de (1821-1890). A Swiss artist who frequently exhibited at the Salon and whose works - generally representing animals - appeared at the First Impressionist Exhibition.

MULOT-DURIVAGE Emilien (1836-?). An inhabitant of Normandy and a participant in the First Impressionist Exhibition.

OTTIN Auguste (1811-1890). A prize-winning (Prix de Rome) sculptor whose works were acclaimed at the Salon. His designs for the sculptures of the Médicis Fountain in the Luxembourg Gardens were shown at the First Impressionist Exhibition.

OTTIN Léon-Auguste (1836-?). The son of Auguste Ottin, he participated in the *Salon des Refusés* and the First and Second Impressionist Exhibitions.

ROBERT Léon-Paul (1849 -?). A student of Puvis de Chavannes and Bonnat, he exhibited his watercolors and *Young Girls in the Hay* at the First Impressionist Exhibition and thereafter participated in the Salons.

SOMM François-Clément (1844-1907). Cartoonist for satirical publications such as *Le Chat Noir* and *Le Rire*. An excellent watercolorist, he took part in the Fourth Impressionist Exhibition and illustrated Goncourt's *La Fille Elisa*.

TILLOT Charles-Victor (1825-1895). Chronicler and art critic at *Le Siècle*. Frequently showed at the Impressionist exhibitions and was an intimate of the Degas circle whose members included the Rouarts, Bartholomé and Mary Cassatt.

VIDAL Eugène (1844-1907). Initially exhibited at the Salon and thereafter at the Impressionist exhibitions of 1880 and 1881.

VIGNON Paul Victor (1847-1909). Vignon's mother was a published author whose reputation facilitated her son's career as an artist. Despite his lackluster reputation, he participated in the final Impressionist exhibitions.

The Godparents

BOUDIN Eugène (1824-1898). A specialist in seascapes, Boudin frequently painted the estuary of the Seine. Baudelaire appreciated his work.

COROT Camille (1796-1875). His manner of representing nature constituted a major revolution in French landscape painting. Without being falsely idealistic, his scenes of peasant life were filled with tenderness and humanity.

DAUBIGNY Charles-François (1817-1878). A painter of landcapes, Daubigny bridged the Barbizon School and the Impressionist movement.

JONGKIND. Johann Barthold (1819-1891). A highly poetic and sensitive Dutch painter who portrayed scenes of rural life and the cycle of the seasons.

MILLET Jean-François (1814-1875). An inspired painter of the unspoiled rural world, he represented peasants with an almost religious dignity.

ROUSSEAU Théodore (1812-1867). A major figure of the Barbizon School, he was chiefly responsible for defining its aesthetic. A lyrical painter of forests and scenes of nature.

The Ancestors

CONSTABLE John (1776-1837). One of the major English romantic painters, celebrated for the dramatic and luminous qualities of his landscapes and skies.

TURNER J.M.William (1775-1851). His audacious style heavily influenced the French painters living in exile in London and paved the way for Impressionism.

The Supporting Roles

BRACQUEMOND Félix (1833-1914). An engraver, Bracquemond was introduced to many of the major writers of the period through Poulet-Malassis, Baudelaire's publisher. He taught Manet the rudiments of engraving and participated in the First Impressionist Exhibition.

CALS Adolphe-Félix (1810-1880). Despite his preference for realism and a more populist approach to his subjects, Cals was associated with the Impressionist movement and participated in several of their exhibitions.

DE NITTIS Giuseppe (1846-1884). A member of the Macchiaioli group in Italy, De Nittis took part in the First Impressionist Exhibition and frequented many of the leading artists and writers of the period, including Degas, Manet, Goncourt, Zola and Daudet. Zola represented him as Fagerolles in his novel *L'Œuvre*.

DESBOUTIN Marcellin (1823-1902). An engraver, Desboutin was a regular at the gatherings at the Café Guerbois and showed at the Second Impressionist Exhibition. His portraits of Goncourt, Degas, Manet and Lepic were characterized by great psychological depth.

FORAIN Jean-Louis (1852-1931). After a bohemian youth spent between the salon of Nina de Callias and the company of Rimbaud, with whom he shared his lodgings, Forain became a chronicler of the foibles of the society of his time and from 1879 participated in all of the Impressionist exhibitions except that of 1882.

GONZALES Eva (1849-1883). The daughter of the journalist Emmanuel Gonzalès and wife of the engraver Henri Guérard. A student of Manet, to whom she was so closely attached that she died five days after his own death.

LEBOURG Albert (1849-1928). Exhibited with the Impressionists in 1879 and 1880. His style was close to their naturalistic and fresh vision of reality. Lebourg was a prolific artist whose works were mainly inspired by Paris and its immediate environs.

LEPIC Ludovic-Napoléon (1839-1889). Encouraged by Degas, who had executed a celebrated portrait of him and his two daughters on the Place de la Concorde, he participated in the First and Second Impressionist Exhibitions. His style was vivacious and elegant.

LÉPINE Stanislas (1835-1892). He participated in the First Impressionist Exhibition; although a low-profile artist, it was said that his work largely contributed "to ruin the academic landscape."

PIETTE Ludovic (1826-1877). Participated in the Third and Fourth Exhibitions. Piette lived in Montfoucault in the Mayenne, where his best friend Pissarro would sometimes come to visit.

RAFFAËLLI Jean-François (1850-1924). Took part in the Impressionist exhibitions of 1880 and 1881. Raffaëlli was particularly admired by J.K. Huysmans, whose texts he illustrated. He forged close relationships with a number of authors of the time, including Mallarmé, Daudet, Goncourt, Champsaur, Mirbeau, Céard, Richepin, Ajalbert and Rosny.

SCHUFFENECKER Claude-Emile (1851-1934). Gauguin's colleague at the Paris stock exchange, he encouraged his friend in his decision to pursue an artistic career. He participated in the last Impressionist exhibition, marked by the disintegration of the movement.

ZANDOMENEGHI Federico (1841-1917). Participated in several Impressionist exhibitions (1879, 1880, 1881, 1886). A member of the Degas clan, he was the object of conflicts which gradually undermined the artistic cohesion of the group.

The Sympathizers

ALEXIS Paul (1847-1901). A naturalist author and boyhood friend of Zola and Cézanne, who portrayed him in *Paul Alexis Reading to Cézanne*. He militated in the press for the replacement of the jury of the Salon, "which presumed to map the paths of talent and railroads of genius." Alexis was also a friend of Doctor Gachet, at whose home in Auvers-sur-Oise he encountered artists such as Pissarro, Murer and Vignon.

ASTRUC Zacharie (1835-1907). A talented sculptor, painter, composer, journalist and poet, Astruc was included in the First Impressionist Exhibition, which he helped to organize. He was portrayed in numerous paintings by artist friends such as Manet, Fantin-Latour and Bazille.

AURIER Georges (1865-1892). An enthusiastic supporter of the second wave of Impressionism, and particularly the works of Gauguin, Aurier wrote the first critical essay on Van Gogh for *Le Mercure de France*.

BANVILLE Théodore de (1823-1891). The author of *Odes funambulesques*, Banville was a friend of Murger, Nadar and Baudelaire. Banville was a frequent client at the Café Guerbois and held a salon frequented by the leading painters and writers of the period. As the art critic for the *National*, he was influential in promoting the Impressionist movement.

BAUDELAIRE Charles (1821-1867). As Manet's friend, he occupied a privileged position as a sympathetic observer of the Impressionist movement, even if he never actually defended it in his writings. One of the leading members of the intelligentsia of the period, he appears in several of Manet's works, including *A Concert in the Tuileries Garden*.

BAZIRE Edmond (1846-1892). The intimate friend of Nina de Callias and a companion of Verlaine and Charles Cros. A regular of the Café Guerbois, Bazire was the author of the first monograph on Manet.

BERGERAT Emile (1845-1923). Théophile Gautier's son-in-law, prolific writer and journalist, Bergerat was the co-founder, with Charpentier, of *La Vie moderne*, a periodical devoted to the art and artists of the period.

BLANCHE Jacques-Emile (1861-1942). He was involved early in the artistic activities of the period, from Impressionism to the universe of Proust.

BURTY Philippe (1830-1890). One of the first to introduce Japanese art in France, Burty was a friend of the Goncourts and a regular of the Nouvelle-Athènes. As a journalist, his judgment of Impressionist artists such as Manet, Degas and Renoir was extremely sure. His novel *Grave Imprudence* was the chronicle of a group of Impressionist painters based on thinly-disguised profiles of Manet, Degas and the artists of the Nouvelle-Athènes café.

CASTAGNARY Jules-Antoine (1830-1888). His epic *Salons*, written from 1857 to 1879, constitutes one of the most amusing chronicles of the social and artistic life of the period.

MENDÈS Catulle (1841-1909). A prolific writer, Gautier's son-in-law and friend of Wagner, Mallarmé, Banville, Rimbaud and Baudelaire.

CAZE Robert (1853-1886). A major figure of the literary scene of his time, Caze was an intimate of Seurat, Pissarro, Signac, Cézanne, Huysmans, Goncourt and Théodor de Wyzewa. He was a regular contributor to *Lutèce* and *La Revue indépendante* and wrote columns for *Le Voltaire* and *Le Réveil*.

CHAMPFLEURY Jules (Husson) (1821-1889). Novelist and defender of Naturalism, a close friend of Courbet and the enthusiastic supporter of Manet. He appears in Fantin-Latour's *Hommage à Delacroix*.

CLADEL Léon (1835-1892). A naturalist writer, regular at the Café Guerbois and friend of Manet, Desboutin, Sisley, Zola and Verlaine.

DAUDET Alphonse (1840-1897). Frequented many of the key Impressionists (Renoir, Manet, Sisley, Monet) less from aesthetic conviction than as a prolongation of his activities as a major author of the period. He often entertained in his country residence of Champrosay, where Delacroix was his neighbor. Edmond de Goncourt died at his home in 1896.

DAYOT Armand (1851-1934). A journalist and art critic, Dayot wrote articles for periodicals such as *Le Figaro*, *Gil Blas* and *Le Temps*, where he was a member of the editorial staff. He organized a retrospective exhibition of Manet's works in 1884 and authored numerous works dealing with art.

DIERX Léon (1838-1912). Poet and member of Nina de Callias' circle he was well-known to Doctor Gachet and the group of artists in Auvers-sur-Oise.

DUJARDIN Edouard (1861-1949). Dujardin was instrumental in introducing the music of Wagner in France. Journalist, essayist and faithful disciple of Mallarmé, Dujardin was an intimate friend of many painters and writers, including Pissarro, Seurat, Anquetin, Guillaumin and Raffaëlli. In *The Laurels Have Been Cut*, one of his best-known novels, he developed a style of interior monologues that prefigured Joyce.

DURANTY Louis Emile (1833-1880). Novelist and author of *The Misfortunes of Henriette Gérard*, Duranty was also an art critic. Degas would paint his portrait.

Duret Théodore (1838-1927). A passionate defender of the Impressionists, Duret was the author of *The History of Impressionist Painters* (1878) and *Avant-Garde* (1885), a collection of critical essays on art.

Ephrussi Charles (1849-1905). Publisher of *La Gazette des Beaux-Arts* and a friend of many of the Impressionist artists (Renoir portrayed him in the *Boater's Luncheon*), Ephrussi was the model for Swann in Proust's *In Remembrance of Things Past*.

Fénéon Félix (1861-1944). Fénéon was intimately involved in the neo-Impressionist adventure. A prolific writer and essayist, he frequented the neo-Impressionist circles and was a close friend of Seurat, whose pointillist techniques he defended in his writings.

Gasquet Joachim (1873-1921). A youthful friend of Cézanne, whose thoughts and observations he noted and later published as a book.

Gautier Théophile (1811-1872). Writer, journalist and author of *Mademoiselle de Maupin* and *Le Capitaine Fracasse*, Gautier was one of the key figures of the bohemian universe of Parisian artists and writers in the latter half of the nineteenth century. Gautier was also a prolific journalist and the author of numerous critical essays on art.

Geffroy Gustave (1855-1926). A novelist (*The Apprentice*) and author of numerous critical essays on art and artists (Constantin Guys, Claude Monet, Daumier). He also wrote about Impressionism in his Parisian chronicles. An early supporter of Cézanne, who painted his portrait.

Goncourt Edmond de (1822-1896) and Jules de (1830-1870). Two brothers whose writings included historical biographies of Madame du Barry and Marie-Antoinette, as well as numerous novels. Following the premature death of his brother Jules, Edmond continued writing naturalistic novels. He was a close friend of many artists and an art critic whose observations appear in his celebrated *Journal*. He also was a privileged witness of the Impressionist movement and inhabited the same neighborhood as the rue Saint-Georges studios frequented by many of the artists who were part of the movement.

Gonzalès Emmanuel (1815-1887). Contributed to *Le Siècle* and founded *La Caricature*. Gonzalès was also a playwright and the author of adventure novels. The father of Eva Gonzalès, he was a close friend of Stevens, Zola and Manet.

Halévy Ludovic (1834-1908). Born into a family of intellectuals active in the cultural life of the period, Halévy collaborated with Meilhac on the librettos of Offenbach's operettas (*La Belle Hélène, La Vie parisienne*). The Halévy townhouse at 22 rue de Douai was the gathering-place for many of the writers and painters of the period. He maintained a long correspondence with Degas, who was a friend and neighbor.

Houssaye Arsène (Housset) (1815-1896). Successively playwright, administrator of the Comédie-Française and museum inspector in the provinces. Active in theatrical circles of the period and an enthusiastic supporter of the Impressionists.

Huysmans Joris Karl (1848-1907). He passed from naturalism to a baroque style in novels such as *A rebours*. Huysmans was also the author of numerous essays on art which were published in the press and later in a volume entitled *L'Art moderne*.

James Henry (1843-1916). Like Proust, his style was a form of literary Impressionism. James was an early supporter of the movement despite his doubts about their second exhibition.

Joyant Maurice (1864-1930). A boyhood friend of Toulouse-Lautrec, he frequented and supported the Impressionists. After Theo Van Gogh, Joyant became the director of the Boussod-Valadon Gallery.

Kahn Gustave (1859-1936). Author of free-verse Symbolist poetry and numerous studies on art and artists of his time. He defended the Impressionists in *La Revue indépendante*. Kahn also became interested in the neo-Impressionists (Seurat, Signac) and the Symbolist painters (Redon, Moreau). He was a member of the circle associated with *La Revue Blanche*.

Lafenestre Georges (1837-1919). A childhood friend of Verlaine and Degas. A supporter of the Macchiaioli movement of Florence, Lafenestre occupied official functions in the government and frequented the painters and writers who gravitated around Nina de Callias and Mallarmé. He militated for the transformation of art and sharply criticized painters such as Ingres and Flandrin.

LAFORGUE Jules (1860-1887). Introduced to the German Imperial Court by Ephrussi, Laforgue became the tutor of the wife of William the First and introduced her to the art of the period. The posthumous publication of *Mélanges* revealed his profound understanding of Impressionist painting, which he considered as "the great melodic voice of the world."

LEMONNIER Camille (1844-1913). An early adept of Impressionism, Lemonnier was an author and novelist who along with Rodenbach, Verhaeren and Le Sidaner promoted Belgian art and culture in his writings.

LESCLIDE Richard (1825-1892). Journalist and novelist, Lesclide contributed to the publication *Paris à l'eau-forte* with Buhot, Carjat, Cladel, Mendès, Monselet, Guérard, Gill and Guillaumin, as well as to Mallarmé's translation of Poe's *The Raven* (illustrated by Manet), *The River* by Charles Cros (illustrated by Manet), and *The Sandalwood Box* also by Charles Cros.

LORRAIN Jean (Paul Duval) (1855-1906). A prolific author who depicted Whistler in *Monsieur de Phocas* and profiled Forain under the pseudonym of Forie. Lorrain was an enthusiastic admirer of Sisley and Monet.

MALLARMÉ Stéphane (1842-1898). One of the major literary figures of his time. Mallarmé's salon at 89 rue de Rome was a center of artistic exchanges between Symbolists, Impressionists and neo-Impressionists. His friendship with Manet and Baudelaire represented the relationship between painting and literature during the period. Mallarmé was portrayed by Manet, Gauguin and Whistler.

MARTELLI Diego (1838-1896). An Italian art critic and defender of the Macchiaioli movement, the precursor of Impressionism in Italy. In Paris, Martelli frequented the Nouvelle-Athènes, where he encountered Manet with Desboutin and Zandomeneghi. He was often painted by artists such as Boldini, Fattori, Zandomeneghi and Degas.

MARX Roger (1859-1913). The friend and companion of writers and artists such as Huysmans, Anatole France, Gide, Arsène Alexandre, Toulouse-Lautrec and Carrière, Marx also collected Impressionist etchings.

MAUPASSANT Guy de (1850-1893). A member of the Médan Group, along with Huysmans, Céard, Hennique, Alexis and Mirbeau. A regular in Impressionist circles, Maupassant's writings were penetrated by the atmosphere of the period.

MAUS Octave (1856-1919). Founder of *L'Art Vivant* in 1881 and active in the organization of the *XX Group* in Brussels. A regular in Symbolist and Impressionist circles.

MEIER-GRAEFE Julius (1867-1935). Founder of *Pan* in Berlin, Meier-Graefe was a key figure in the recognition of Impressionism. He published numerous books dedicated to the movement and its artists, including Monet, Cézanne, Pissarro, Renoir, Gauguin, Toulouse-Lautrec and Degas.

MIRBEAU Octave (1848-1917). Novelist (*Le Jardin des supplices, Journal d'une femme de chambre*), Mirbeau was an energetic supporter of Impressionism, which he defended in numerous articles.

MONFREID Georges-Daniel de (1856-1929). A friend of Gauguin, with whom he maintained a rich and ongoing correspondence, and for whose recognition he fought following the painter's death.

MOORE George (1852-1933). An Irish novelist, Moore witnessed the birth of Impressionism and was a faithful client at the Nouvelle-Athènes. Manet executed his portrait; he also appears in Degas' *The Absinthe Drinker*.

MOREAU-NÉLATON Etienne (1859-1927). A wealthy patron of the arts and the author of critical essays on the works of Corot, Fantin-Latour, Millet, Daubigny, Jongkind, Manet and Delacroix.

MORICE Charles (1861-1919). Art critic and novelist, Morice contributed to numerous periodicals. An admirer of Mallarmé and Verlaine, he was one of the first to acclaim the works of artists such as Whistler, Pissarro, Fantin-Latour, Gauguin and Cézanne.

NOUVEAU Germain (1851-1920). A member of the "Vilains Bonshommes" group along with Rimbaud, Cros, Verlaine, Gill and Carjat. He visited London with Rimbaud, was a close friend of Forain and frequented the salon of Nina de Callias.

PÉLADAN Josephin (Sâr Péladan) (1859-1918). A prolific writer and author of *La Décadence latine* and *Le Vice suprême*. He militated against artistic realism in *L'Art ochlocratique*; his attitude toward the Impressionists was ambiguous and he clearly preferred Symbolist artists like Moreau.

PICARD Edmond (1836-1924). Founder of a magazine dedicated to modern art to which Verhaeren and Huysmans contributed. Worked with Maus for the recognition of Belgian art, participated in the exhibitions of the *XX Group* and the *Libre Esthétique* which was sympathetic to the Impressionist cause.

PROUST Antonin (1832-1905). A close friend of Manet and a journalist at *La Revue Blanche*. As a member of the government, his official position enabled him to further the careers of many of the Impressionist artists.

PROUST Marcel (1871-1922). In his enormous fresco, *In Remembrance of Things Past*, the painter Elstir was the composite of Helleu, Monet, Whistler and Renoir, with additional elements taken from the lives of Degas, Renoir, Gervex and Blanche. His manner of writing was the literary counterpart of the decomposition of images practiced by the Impressionist painters.

RÉGNIER Henri de (1864-1936). A Symbolist poet, Régnier also wrote for periodicals and the press. A staunch supporter of the neo-Impressionist painters as well as Whistler, Redon and Berthe Morisot.

RENARD Jules (1864-1910). One of the founders of the *Mercure de France*. Celebrated for his caustic *Journal* and plays, which included *Poil de Carotte*, *Le Plaisir de rompre* and *Le Pain de ménage*. He frequented the Symbolist artists and wrote critical essays on Cézanne, Renoir and Lautrec.

RIMBAUD Arthur (1854-1891). Although he was less than enthusiastic about the painting of his time, he nevertheless encountered Manet, Bazille, Verlaine and Fantin-Latour, who portrayed him in *Around the Table*.

RIVIÈRE Georges (1855-1943). A regular of the Impressionist studios, and particularly that of Renoir on the rue Saint-Georges, Rivière published a small Impressionist magazine during the Third Exhibition. His daughters married Renoir's nephew and Cezanne's son.

ROLLINAT Maurice (1846-1903). George Sand's grandson, member of the "Vilains Bonshommes" and a regular at the Chat Noir. In *Les Névrosés*, Rollinat gave the full measure of his taste for the macabre. He was also a close friend of Monet, who was a guest in his country house in the center of France.

RUSKIN John (1819-1900). An illustration of the subtle relationship between art and literature relative to Impressionism. Ruskin's best-known works (*The Seven Lamps of Architecture* and *The Stones of Venice*) had a great influence on the artistic life of the period. His *Bible of Amiens*, translated by Marcel Proust, became a definitive work on the subject of the mysteries of creation.

SEGALEN Victor (1878-1919). An intimate of the Symbolist artists and writers (Huysmans, Remy de Gourmont), Segalen was an avid archaeologist - specializing in Oriental civilizations - and a writer (*Stèles*). He was also an enthusiastic admirer of Gauguin, who inspired his novel *Les Immémoriaux*, published under the pseudonym of Max Ariely.

SILVESTRE Armand (1837-1901). Civil-servant, writer, and friend of numerous poets including Verlaine, Mendès and Valade. Silvestre was an early enthusiast of Impressionism, which he defended in his writings. In his *Land of Memories*, he evoked La Nouvelle-Athenes and the beginnings of Impressionism.

STRINDBERG August (1849-1912). Swedish playwright and novelist, Strindberg authored works such as *Miss Julie*, *The Dance of Death*, *Inferno* and *The Ghost Sonata*. He also dabbled in painting, encouraged by his friend Edward Munch. In terms of style, a parallel can be drawn between his writings and certain principles of Impressionist art.

TABARANT Adolphe (1863-1950). Art critic and historian (*The True Visage of Restif de la Bretonne*), he shared the bohemian existence of the Impressionist artists who lived at the Château des Brouillards in Montmartre. Tabarant was the author of books on the Impressionist movement and artists such as Pissarro, Manet and Luce.

TAINE Hippolyte (1828-1893). Philosopher, historian (*The Origins of Contemporary France*) and author of *Parisian Life*, a bitter, modern chronicle of urban existence which evoked the visions of Degas, Cassatt and Manet. Taine had first encountered the Impressionists during his visits to Barbizon. Like Zola, he would progressively lose his enthusiasm for the movement.

THORÉ Théophile (1807-1869). In his chronicles devoted to the Salon, his perception of the new movement of Impressionism was particularly lucid. He was one of the first critics to review the works of Degas, Bazille, Renoir and Pissarro.

Valabrègue Antony (1844-1900). A member of the small circle of artists and writers in Aix which included Zola, Cézanne and Paul Alexis. Poet, art critic and journalist, he was portrayed in Zola's novel *L'Œuvre*; Cézanne also executed his portrait.

Valéry Paul (1871-1945). Intimately linked to the circle of Berthe Morisot, Valéry married her niece. He chronicled the life of Degas in *Degas, danse, dessins*, and was among the poets who frequented Mallarmé's salon. Valéry was a childhood friend of Pierre Louÿs and André Gide. He was also the author of numerous texts on Impressionist painters.

Verhaeren Emile (1855-1916). Through his Belgian origins, Verhaeren was a friend of Symbolist and neo-Impressionist painters like Théo Van Rysselberghe. He also courageously defended Seurat during the period when he was under attack by the art establishment.

Verlaine Paul (1844-1896). Verlaine was not directly connected to the Impressionist movement even though his poetry reflected its spirit. Verlaine was a close friend of Rimbaud, Forain, Mallarmé, Aman-Jean (to whom he dedicated his poems), Carrière, Steinlen (who painted his portrait) and Gauguin. He was also an intimate of the circle of Nina de Callias.

Wilde Oscar (1854-1900). One of the key figures of the cultural life of the period.

Wyzewa Theodor (de Wyzewski) (1862-1917). Of Polish origins, he was one of the principal intermediaries between the Parisian avant-garde and European cultural centers. With Dujardin, he was the co-founder of the *Revue wagnérienne* and collaborated on numerous publications for which he wrote articles on Boudin, Renoir, Degas and Mallarmé, whose Tuesday-afternoon salons on the rue de Rome he regularly frequented. His articles on art and painting were published under the titles *Nos Maîtres* and *Peintres de jadis et d'aujourd'hui*.

Zola Emile (1840-1902). A great deal of ambiguity surrounds the attitude of the author of *Rougon-Macquart*. In *Mon salon*, Zola courageously defended Impressionism through its principal representative, Manet. Despite his childhood friendship with Cézanne and his relations with other Impressionist artists, his novel *L'Œuvre* was highly critical of the movement. Many of Zola's novels are marked by his intimate knowledge of Impressionist painters; like Maupassant, he drew his inspiration from the same places and often the same individuals.

The Next Generation

Gauguin Paul (1848-1903). Although he showed in the Impressionist exhibitions beginning in 1879, he troubled (like Seurat) the original spirit of the movement. Strong-willed, intransigent and egocentric, Gauguin was a natural-born leader and a source of artistic innovation. An instrumental member of the Pont-Aven group, Gauguin would finish his days in the voluptuous solitude of Tahiti.

Redon Odilon (1840-1916). His emotional distance and originality made his integration into the Impressionist movement impossible. He only participated in the Eighth Exhibition, during the decline of the movement. Mallarmé's admiration for his work was based on the subtle relationship between art and literature, for only the poet is capable of bridging the diversity represented by artists like Manet, Morisot, Renoir, Gauguin, Gustave Moreau or Whistler.

Seurat Georges (1859-1891). The founding father of Pointillism, a movement based on the science of colors that transcended the aesthetic principles of the Impressionists.

Signac Paul (1863-1935). Initially influenced by Seurat, he also showed at the Eighth and last Impressionist exhibition. In the years which followed, he gradually emerged from Seurat's shadow and became an important and original contributor to the painting of his period.

Toulouse-Lautrec Henri de (1864-1901). His aristocratic origins and physical infirmity made him a singular figure on the Parisian art scene of the period. His art was original, daring and innovative, although he attracted far fewer disciples or imitators than either Cézanne or Van Gogh. Toulouse-Lautrec was as much an artist of life than of paint and canvas.

Van Gogh Vincent (1853-1890). Incomparably original and condemned to an existence of poverty, misunderstanding and isolation, even his idealistic dream of an artists' co-operative with Gauguin turned into a nightmare. His suicide in a field under the burning summer's sun has inscribed his legend and martyrdom for eternity.

The Salons

ANDRÉE Ellen (?). Served as Manet's model for *La Prune* and also modeled for Gervex, Renoir and Stevens. Degas immortalized her in *L'Absinthe*, in which she appears with Desboutin. She ultimately became a member of Antoine's theater company and pursued a successful career as an actress.

AROSA (family). Achille and Gustave were two patrons of the arts who played an important role in the destiny of Gauguin, whom they financially supported during his early years as a painter.

AVRIL Jane (1868-1923). One of Toulouse-Lautrec's favorite models. Vivacious and provocative, her legendary silhouette represented by Lautrec became the symbol of the universe of Parisian music halls of the late nineteenth century.

BELLIO Georges de (1828-1894). A physician, patron of the arts and friend of many of the most important Impressionist painters. His collection was reputed to include Monet's legendary *Impression, soleil levant*, one of the first Impressionist works.

BÉRARD (family). Close friends of Renoir who was a frequent guest at the château de Wargemont, their country estate. The Bérard family also possessed an important collection of Impressionist works, including paintings by Monet and Morisot.

BEURDELEY Alfred (1847-1919). The son of a rich family of industrialists, his collection of Impressionist paintings included works by Sisley, Lépine and Manet.

BIBESCO Georges (1834-1902). Art lover and collector. Proust would study the behavior of the painters and the members of Parisian high society that frequented his townhouse at 22 boulevard de Latour-Maubourg.

BING Samuel (1838-1905). Introduced Oriental art into France. His gallery, initially located at 19 rue Chauchat and later at 22 rue de Provence, became fashionable through the influence of Philippe Burty and the Goncourt brothers. Bing was responsible for launching Japanese art in France, and played an important role in the aesthetic development of the Impressionist movement.

BLOT Eugène (1857-?). Collector and art dealer. The author of *Histoire d'une collection de tableaux modernes ou cinquante ans de peinture* (A History of a Modern Art Collection, or Fifty Years of Painting). His prestigious collection included works by Degas, Guillaumin, Manet, Pissarro, Morisot, Renoir, Sisley and Gauguin.

BONNIÈRES (1850-1905). A key figure of Parisian social and artistic life of the period. An art and music lover, he traveled to Bayreuth for Wagner's operas and attended the exhibition of the *XX Group* in Brussels. In Paris, he held a salon at 26 rue de Condé in the former Beaumarchais townhouse, which would later become the editorial offices of the newspaper *Mercure de France*.

BOUSSOD-VALADON, Gallery. The main gallery showed works by academic artists. The second, located at 19 boulevard Montmartre, promoted the Impressionists and other avant-garde artists of the period. Vincent's brother Theo Van Gogh was briefly the director of the latter gallery.

CABANER François (Matt) (1833-1881). A composer who set texts by the poets Mallarmé and Baudelaire to music. An early friend and supporter of the Impressionists; Chabrier, Richepin, Rollinat, Verlaine, Renoir, Forain and Cézanne regularly frequented his apartment on the rue Fontaine.

CADAR Alfred (1828-1875). A publisher of art books and the founder of the French Watercolorist Association, whose headquarters where located in his editorial offices at 66 rue de Richelieu. Works by Bracquemond, Manet and Jongkind were regularly reproduced in his periodicals.

CALLIAS Nina de (Nina de Villard) (1845-1884). Her salon at 17 rue Chaptal and later at 82 rue des Moines was frequented by the cream of the Parisian literary and artistic world. Charles Cros dedicated *Le Coffret de santal (The Sandalwood Box)* to her. The "princess of bohemians" according to Léo Larguier, she was the first to receive Rimbaud and Verlaine. Catulle Mendès portrayed her as the heroine of his novel, *La Maison de la vieille* (The Old Woman's House).

CAMONDO Isaac comte de (1851-1911). Banker and enlightened collector whose apartment near the Paris Opera contained works by Boudin, Cézanne, Manet, Van Gogh, Monet, Pissarro and Toulouse-Lautrec.

CARJAT Etienne (1828-1906). Cartoonist, journalist and photographer, Carjat would employ all of these media to portray the members of the Paris intelligentsia of the period. His works included striking portraits of Nerval, Baudelaire and Rimbaud.

CASSIRER Paul (1871-1926). Introduced Impressionism into Germany.

CHABRIER Emmanuel (1841-1894). A musician, Chabrier often posed for his painter friends James Tissot, Fantin-Latour, Manet and Degas.

CHARPENTIER Georges (1846-1901). The most fashionable editor of his period, Charpentier published texts by Daudet, Maupassant, Zola and Goncourt. His townhouse on the rue de Grenelle was the site of one of the most popular and brilliant salons in Paris.

CHOCQUET Victor (1821-1891). A discreet employee of the French Ministry of Finance and independently wealthy, Chocquet was the perfect example of the enlightened collector and patron of the arts. Cézanne did his portrait.

CLEMENCEAU Georges (1841-1929). A physician, senior statesman and author of a book about Monet. Clemenceau was instrumental in the acquisition of Monet's *Water Lilies* for the Orangerie Museum of Paris.

DESOYE. The owner of La Porte chinoise, 220 rue de Rivoli. The celebrated shop helped popularize Oriental art in France and was frequented by artists and writers such as Zola, Champfleury, Manet, Degas, Duranty, Tissot, Monet, Bracquemond and Fantin-Latour.

DEUDON Charles (1832-1914). The very sociable owner of the Old England clothing store in Paris, Deudon frequently attended the Impressionist dinners organized at the Café Riche.

DIHAU (family). Désiré (who played bassoon in the orchestra of the Paris Opera), Henri (a music composer) and Marie (soloist at the Concerts Lamoureux) were close friends of Degas who portrayed them in *Les Musiciens à l'orchestre* (The Musicians of the Orchestra) and Toulouse-Lautrec who painted the *Portrait of Mademoiselle Dihau at the Piano*.

DORIA Armand (1824-1896). An important patron of the arts and collector of Impressionist works, including Cézanne's *La Maison du pendu* (*The House of the Hanged Man*).

DURAND-RUEL Paul (1831-1922). Gallery-owner and key figure in the Impressionist movement. The son of an art dealer, Durand-Ruel was an early supporter of the Barbizon painters Millet, Courbet and Corot. As the champion of the Impressionists, he fiercely defended them in France and promoted their works in the United States.

EVANS Thomas (1823-1897). An intimate of the Imperial Court, his financial support of his mistress 'Mery' Laurent permitted the latter to create a salon frequented by artists and writers such as Mallarmé, Manet, Degas, Huysmans and Whistler.

FAURE Jean-Baptiste (1830-1914). A famous period baritone whose collection of Impressionist works included paintings by Degas, Manet, Monet, Pissarro and Sisley.

FEYDEAU Georges (1862-1921). A popular playwright whose light theatrical works included *L'Hôtel du Libre échange, Le Dindon* and *Occupe-toi d'Amélie* (The Hotel of Free Exchange; The Turkey; Take Care of Amelia). His princely royalties enabled him to create an outstanding art collection.

FOURNAISE Alphonse. The owner of a restaurant in the riverside village of Chatou, popular with students and artists. The restaurant served as the backdrop to Renoir's *Le Déjeuner des canotiers* (*The Boaters' Luncheon*).

FRY Roger (1866-1934). An English painter and art critic, Fry frequented both the Impressionist painters in France and later the Bloomsbury Group in London, whose members included Lytton Strachey and Virginia Woolf. He was among the first to consider Cézanne as the father of modern painting.

GACHET Paul (1828-1909). Doctor, art collector and accomplished engraver (Cézanne was briefly his student), Gachet's friends included several of the most talented artists and writers of the period, many of whom frequented his country home in Auvers-sur-Oise. He is probably best remembered for his relationship with Vincent Van Gogh, whom he befriended and attempted to treat during the months preceding his suicide.

GAUDIBERT (family). Residents of Le Havre on the coast of Normandy, the Gaudiberts were close friends of the painter Boudin and actively supported the early efforts of Monet, who would paint the *Portrait of Madame Gaudibert*.

GAUTIER Judith (1850-1917). The daughter of Théophile Gautier and future wife of Catulle Mendès. Highly cultured, she was an enthusiastic admirer of Wagner and Japanese art. Although initially hostile to the Impressionist movement, her circle of friends included several of its members.

GODEBSKA Marie (Misia) (1872-1950). The Muse of *La Revue Blanche*. The contributing artists and writers of the magazine, which was published by her husband Thadée Natanson, were frequent guests at the couple's Paris residence on the rue de Prony and their country house in the village of Villeneuve-sur-Yonne.

HAVEMEYER Louise (1858-1929) An early friend of Mary Cassatt, who introduced her to many of the Impressionist painters. Married to a wealthy American, her collection of works by Manet, Monet, Cézanne, Pissarro and Degas was the largest in the United States. After her death, the paintings were bequeathed to the Metropolitan Museum of New York, becoming the core of its Impressionist collection. .

HAVILAND Charles (1839-1921). Son of the founder of a porcelain studio in Limoges, whose Paris outlet was headed by the painter Bracquemond. Haviland's collection of Impressionist paintings included Manet's *Jockeys Before the Race* and *The Barmaid* by Degas.

HECHT (family). Henri and Albert Hecht often accompanied Degas on his backstage visits to the Paris Opera and appear in several of his paintings.

HOSCHEDÉ Alice (1844-1911). The wife of a wealthy merchant who opened their chateau to period painters and writers. Losing his fortune, her husband became a journalist; after his death, Alice married the painter Monet, whose own wife had died.

HOWLAND Hortense (1835-1920). A member of Parisian high society, her salon was frequented by members of the Jockey Club as well as by artists such as Fromentin, Bartholomé, Helleu, Mary Cassatt and Robert de Montesquiou. Marcel Proust encountered Charles Hass, the model for Proust's fictional character Swann, at her home.

KRÖLLER-MÜLLER. Wife of A.G. Kröller, a Dutch businessman whose extensive collection of Impressionist paintings was donated to the museum she founded in Holland that bears her name.

LA GANDARA Antonio (1862-1917). Like Stevens and Boldini, La Gandara was a well-connected society painter. His studio on the rue Monsieur le Prince was frequented by a select group of aristocrats, artists and writers; Proust based several of his fictional characters on the individuals who frequented his salon.

LATHUILLE. The owner of the restaurant of the same name located on boulevard de Clichy. Both the restaurant and the nearby Café Guerbois were popular gathering-places for many artists and writers of the period.

LAURENT Anne-Rose (Mery) (1849-1900). The mistress of Thomas Evans. The gatherings at her residence at 9 boulevard Lannes were frequented by many of the most brilliant artists and writers of the period.

LE BARC DE BOUTEVILLE (1837-1897). An art dealer and close friend of Pissarro.

LECADRE Marie-Jeanne (1790-1870). Claude Monet's aunt and an early and enthusiastic supporter of the artist.

LECLANCHÉ Maurice (?-1921). One of the first to collect Manet's works, as well as paintings by Gauguin, Signac, Mary Cassatt, Guillaumin, Pissarro, Monet, Sisley and Toulouse-Lautrec.

LE CŒUR Charles (1830-1906). A close friend of Renoir, he appears in the *Cabaret de la mère Anthony* and in many of his portraits.

LEJOSNE Hippolyte (1814-1884). A career officer in the French army and intimate friend of the Guerbois family. His residence at 6 avenue Trudaine was a gathering-place for artists and writers such as Manet, Baudelaire, Constantin Guys, Bracquemond, Stevens and Astruc.

LEMAIRE Madeleine (1845-1928). Hosted famous salons on the rue de Monceau and at the Château de Réveillon which attracted brilliant representatives from Parisian society and the fine arts. It was at these celebrated gatherings that Marcel Proust would find the models for many of the characters of *In Remembrance of Things Past*.

LEROLLE Henry (1848-1929). Painter, patron of the arts and noted collector of Impressionist works. A music lover, Lerolle organized concerts by Vincent d'Indy and Debussy which were attended by Renoir, Degas, Forain, Mallarmé, Claudel and Gide. His daughters married into the Rouart family.

LUGNÉ-POE Aurélien (1869-1940). Founded the *Théâtre de l'Œuvre*. He was a central figure among the artists of the generation that succeeded Impressionism, and a friend of Alfred Jarry. His studio at 28 rue Pigalle was a veritable laboratory of the arts.

MAITRE Edmond (1840-1898). A close friend of Bazille, Renoir and Fantin-Latour, who portrayed him in the *Studio of the rue La Condamine* and *Around the Piano*.

MARTIN Pierre Ferdinand (Père Martin). A small independent art dealer and owner of a bric-a-brac shop located first on the rue de Clichy and thereafter at 52 rue Laffitte. Martin had been a day-laborer and an extra in theatrical productions before opening his shop, which functioned as an unofficial showcase for the early Impressionist painters.

MAY Ernest (1845-1925). Initially collected pre-Impressionist works. A friend of both Manet and Degas, who portrayed him in *At the Stock Market*. His collection included works by Monet, Sisley, Pissarro and Renoir.

MEURENT Victorine. As Manet's favorite model, she posed for *Olympia* and *The Street Singer* and is the central figure in *Déjeuner sur l'herbe*. Following a brief career as an actress, she began painting and exhibited her works at the Salon.

MEURICE (Madame Paul) (1819-1874). The wife of Victor Hugo's most faithful disciple, her artistic and literary gatherings on the avenue Frochot were frequented by Manet, Champfleury, Fantin-Latour, Astruc and Stevens.

MONTESQUIOU Robert de (1855-1921). His tastes ran to Whistler and the minor Impressionists. Influential because of his social position and highly intelligent, he made a lasting impression on Marcel Proust.

MURER Hyacinthe (Eugène Meunier) (1846-1906). After engaging in a variety of professions and briefly participating in the anarchist movement, Murer published several novels under the pseudonym of Gêne-Mur. He went on to open a restaurant at 95 boulevard Voltaire which became a gathering-place for the Impressionists, whose works he collected. In 1881 he left Paris for Rouen, where he became the owner of the Hotel du Dauphin et d'Espagne, often frequented by his painter friends.

NADAR (Félix Tournachon) (1820-1910). Journalist, cartoonist and pioneer photographer, Nadar was always at the center of the cultural activity of his era. The First Impressionist Exhibition was held in his studio on the boulevard des Capucines.

NATANSON Thadée (1868-1951). Businessman and Misia's first husband. A familiar of many writers and artists of the period, from Mallarmé to Anatole France, Proust, Mirbeau, Pissarro and Gauguin. Author of a book of profiles and character studies of many of his friends and acquaintances.

PAGANS Lorenzo (?-1884). Often portrayed by Degas in his paintings of musical subjects. A regular at the evening gatherings of Manet, Dihau and De Nittis.

PETIT Gallery. After promoting the artists of the School of 1830, the gallery represented the Impressionists. Located on the corner of the rues de Sèze and Godot-de-Moroy, the gallery internationalized its activities and became a hub for the most contemporary artistic movements in France and other countries.

PORTIER Alphonse ((?-1902). Originally the owner of a bric-a-brac shop on rue Notre-Dame-de-Lorette, Portier was an early supporter of the Impressionists and participated in the organization of their exhibitions.

PRINS Pierre (1838-1913). He appears in Manet's *Le Balcon* and became the husband of Fanny Claus, who was also represented in the painting. His works were not shown at the First Impressionist Exhibition due to the negligence of a friend who was supposed to give them to Sisley. Prins helped organize international exhibitions at the Petit Gallery.

ROUART Henri (1833-1912). A wealthy manufacturer and painter who showed at the Impressionist exhibitions. His townhouse on the rue de Lisbonne was frequented by writer and painter friends. Degas, who often dined there, represented Rouart in many of his paintings. His private collection was one of the most important holdings of Impressionist works. His son Ernest (1874-1942) married Julie Manet, the daughter of Berthe Morisot and Eugène Manet. The couple inhabited a townhouse belonging to Julie's mother, which they shared with Gobillart and Paul Valéry.

SEGATORI Agostina. Vincent Van Gogh painted her portrait and exhibited his collection of Japanese prints in her café (le Tambourin) on the avenue de Clichy. The café also hosted an exhibition of Van Gogh's own works as well as those of Toulouse-Lautrec and Anquetin.

STCHOUKINE Sergeï (1851-1936). Along with Morosov, he was one of the most active collectors of modern art. His salon on the avenue de Wagram received writers and artists such as Degas, Huysmans and Renoir.

TANGUY Julien-François (Le Père Tanguy) (1825-1894). A paint merchant and grassroots anarchist, Tanguy was a regular visitor to Barbizon and a friend of many of the Impressionists. His shop at 14 rue Clauzel was a gathering-place for artists (Van Gogh first encountered Cézanne there) and an unofficial gallery for their works, which he often acquired in exchange for paints, brushes and canvas.

THÉRÉSA (Emma Valadon) (1837-1913). Café singer and model for artists such as Manet and Degas, who portrayed her in *La Chanteuse au chien*.

VALTESSE DE LA BIGNE (Lucie Delabigne) (1859-1910). Following a career as an actress playing minor roles, she became a celebrated courtesan. Her residence at 98 boulevard Malesherbes was frequented by the cream of the artistic and literary world. Her legendary bed was described by Zola in his novel *Nana*.

VEVER Henri (1885-1942). Famous Paris jeweler and author of a history of 19th-century jewelry. Vever collected Oriental art and possessed a country house near Monet's residence in Giverny. His wealth permitted him to assemble an important collection of works by Corot, Boudin, Fantin-Latour, Monet, Pissarro, Renoir and Sisley. .

VIAU Georges (1855-1939). A wealthy and socially well-connected dentist, Viau's excellent collection included works by Boudin, Cassatt, Cézanne, Degas, Guillaumin, Manet, Monet, Renoir and Sisley.

WIDENER Peter (1834-1915). After having amassed a fortune in the railroad business in the United States, Widener assembled an important collection of Impressionist works, including *Les Régates d'Argenteuil* by Monet, *Marly-le-Roi* by Sisley, *Le Toréro mort* by Manet, *Aux courses* and *Le Foyer de l'Opera* by Degas and *La Danseuse* by Renoir.

International Impressionism

ANCHER Anna (1859-1935). The daughter of a hotel owner in Skagen (Denmark), where an artists' colony had also been established. Ancher habitually portrayed scenes inspired by her immediate environment.

ANDRESCU Ion (1850-1882). A Hungarian painter from Bucharest, Andrescu joined the artists living in Barbizon in 1880.

BENSON Frank Weston (1862-1951). An art teacher in Boston and a pioneer of Impressionist art in America.

BIRGER Hugo (1854-1889). Worked with Josephson and lived in Paris from 1879 to 1881.

Breck John Leslie (1860-1899) After numerous visits to Europe and Paris (1886-87), Breck joined the American artists' colony in Giverny.

BRUCE William Blair (1859-1906). An American artist who lived in the south of France. After marrying a Swedish sculptress, he settled in Sweden.

CHASE William Merritt (1849-1916). A friend of Stevens and Whistler, Chase taught in the United States after frequenting the Impressionists in Paris.

CLAUSEN George (1852-1944). An adept of Impressionism, Clausen transformed the way in which art was taught in England. A joint-founder of the "New English Art Club."

CORINTH Lovis (1858-1925). Along with Liebermann and Slevogt, he helped popularise Impressionism in Germany.

FATTORI Giovanni (1825-1908). One of the key members of the Macchiaioli movement.

FERENCZY Karoly (1862-1917). After a stay in Paris (1887-1889), Ferenczy became one of the leading proponents of Impressionism in Hungary.

HASSAM Childe (1859-1935). Courted the Impressionist painters at the Café Guerbois and later transposed their techniques to his native America.

HILL Carl (1849-1911). Of Swedish origin, Hill lived and painted in Barbizon (1874). Although he was slated to exhibit his works at the Third Impressionist Exhibition, his paintings were never displayed. Hill's life terminated in madness.

HODLER Ferdinand (1853-1918). Hodler's career as a painter was varied and included a period heavily influenced by Impressionism.

JOHANSEN Vigo (1851-1935). Frequented Manet during his sojourn in Paris in 1880; his painting reflects their encounter.

JOSEPHSON Ernst (1851-1906). Lived in Paris with Carl Hill and travelled in Europe before settling in Sweden.

KROHG Christian (1852-1925). A key figure in the contacts between Scandinavian artists and Paris, Krohg encountered and was influenced by the Impressionists. As an artist, he alternated between their style and social realism.

KRÖYER Peder Severin (1851-1909). Settled in Skagen and painted with Krohg, Anna Ancher and Johansen.

LARSSON Carl (1853-1919). A Swedish painter who inhabited Grez-sur-Loing. Larsson would later return to Sweden where he pursued a successful career as an illustrator.

LA THANGUE Henry Herbert (1859-1929). Closely linked to the Impressionists, whose themes he adapted to his own style.

LEGA Silvestro (1826-1895). An active member of the movement for the unification of Italy, Lega also participated in the Macchiaioli movement.

LEVITAN Isaac (1861-1900). Exiled from Moscow because of his religion (Levitan was Jewish), he voyaged through Europe and sojourned on the banks of the Volga, the inspiration of his luminous and vibrant landscapes.

LIEBERMANN Max (1847-1935). A major German artist of the period. Liebermann inhabited Barbizon (1874-1877) before returning to Germany and living in Munich and Berlin.

MORRICE James Wilson (1865-1924). A Canadian painter who lived at Grez-sur-Loing and Pont-Aven. His manner was similar to Boudin's.

PAAL Lazlo (1846-1879). Sojourned in Barbizon from 1872-1879.

PHILIPSEN Theodor (1840-1920). Helped organise the first impressionist exhibitions. Philipsen was influenced by Manet and Pissarro; he would later encounter Gauguin in Denmark.

REGOYOS Y VALDES Dario (1857-1913). Co-founder of the *XX Group* in Brussels. Frequented Whistler, Pissarro, Degas and Seurat. Regoyos participated in Pointillist movement and the circle of artists that gravitated around the *Revue Blanche* magazine.

RÉPINE Ilia (1844-1930). Encountered Zola in Paris (1876) and traveled widely throughout Europe and the Middle-East. Successively lived in Moscow, Saint Petersburg and on his estate at Kuokkala where he died.

ROBINSON Théodore (1852-1896). A pioneer of Impressionism in the United States, Robinson frequently visited Monet in Giverny.

SARGENT John Singer (1856-1925). The son of an American physician established in Europe, Sargent was born in Florence, studied in Rome and Paris, and lived in Spain and Holland before settling in England, where he pursued a brilliant career as a society painter.

SEROV Valentin (1865-1911). Serov painted in the Ukraine with Répine and participated with Levitan in the exhibitions of the Itinerants.

SICKERT Walter (1860-1942). Studied under Whistler, encountered Degas and participated in the circle of artists that formed around Jacques-Emile Blanche in Dieppe.

SIGNORINI Telemaco (1835-1901). Signorini participated in the activities of the Macchiaioli group and was influenced by Degas.

SLEVOGT Max (1868-1932). A member of the Succession group of Munich, Slevogt bridged Impressionism and various avant-garde movements which followed.

STARR Sydney (1857-1925). Similar in manner to Whistler, Starr exhibited at the "New English Art Club" and with the English Impressionists.

STEER Philip Wilson (1860-1942). Studied in the Paris art schools and was influenced by the Impressionists. A founding member of the "New English Art Club."

THAULOW Fritz (1847-1906). Gauguin's brother-in-law (his wife was Mette Gauguin's sister), Thaulow painted naturalistic works in Norway with Krohg. Strindberg would begin his autobiographical novel *Inferno* at Thaulow's home in Dieppe.

WHISTLER James Abbott (1834-1903). An artist whose life and career spanned Paris and London, Whistler exhibited at the *Salon des Refusés* and maintained a series of professional and social ties with many of the Impressionists, including Fantin-Latour.

Chronology

1863: The *Salon des Refusés*. Carpeaux: *Ugolin* - Fromentin: *Falcon Hunt in Algeria* - Puvis de Chavannes: *Work, Le Repos* - Cabanel: *The Birth of Venus* - Courbet: *La Treille* - Millet: *La Cardeuse de laine, L'Homme à la houe* - Manet: *Le Déjeuner sur l'herbe.*
Hittorf: Architect of the Gare du Nord Railway Station, Paris.
Gautier: *Le Capitaine Fracasse* - Fromentin: *Dominique* - Renan: *The Life of Jesus* - Baudelaire: *Petits Poèmes en prose.*
Smetana: *Les Brandebourgeois en Bohême* - Berlioz: *Les Troyens* - Bizet: *The Pearl-Divers.*
Death of Delacroix, J. Grimm, Thackeray and Vigny.
Insurrection in Poland - Maximilien the First Emperor of Mexico - French domination of Cambodia.

1864: Cabanel, Gérôme and Corot serve on the jury of the Salon. The Atelier Gleyre closes; Monet, Renoir, Sisley and Bazille discover Barbizon. Monet, Jongkind and Boudin visit Normandy and paint in Honfleur and Sainte-Adresse.
Meissonier: *1814, Napoleon III at the Battle of Solferino* - Boecklin: *Villa on the Sea* - Millet: *Shepherdess with Her Flock* - Gustave Moreau: *Oedipus and the Sphinx* - Courbet: *Le Réveil* - Corot: *The Road to Sèvres* Fantin-Latour: *Homage to Delacroix.*
Davioud: Architect of the theatres on the Place du Châtelet (Paris).
Goncourt: *Renée Mauperin* - Erckmann-Chatrian: *L'Ami Fritz* - Labiche: *La Cagnotte* - Zola: *Les Contes à Ninon* - Fustel de Coulanges: *La Cité antique.*
Gounod: *Mireille* - Offenbach: *La Belle Hélène* - Berlioz: *The Damnation of Faust.*
Death of Flandrin, Hawthorne and Meyerber.
The First Workers' International founded. - Creation of the Red Cross.

1865: Manet's *Olympia* creates a scandal. Corot encounters Boudin, Whistler and Courbet in Normandy.
Courbet: *Proudhon* - Henner: *The Chaste Suzanne* - Boudin: *Empress Eugénie on the Beach at Trouville* - Whistler: *Girl in White* - Ribot: *The Martyr of Saint Sebastien* - Degas: *The Sorrows of the City of Orleans* - Monet: *Le Déjeuner sur l'herbe.*
Mengoni: architect of the Gallery Victor-Emmanuel in Milan.
Goncourt: *Germinie Lacerteux* - Jules Verne: *Voyage to the Moon* - Taine: *The Philosophy of Art* - Barbey d'Aurevilly: *A Married Priest* - Lewis Carroll: *Alice in Wonderland.*
Rimski-Korsakov: *First Symphony.*
Civil War ends in the United States; slavery is abolished - Assassinations of Abraham Lincoln and of the Duke of Morny.

1866: Renoir retreats to the village of Marlotte (at the Auberge of the Mère Anthony) - Pissarro moves to Pontoise.
Carpeaux: *The Triumph of Flore* - Courbet: *Sleep* and *Woman with Parrot* - Renoir: *Le Cabaret de la mère Anthony* - Manet: *Le Fifre* - Degas: *At the Race Track* - Cézanne: *Portrait of his Father Reading* - Bazille: *The Family Reunion.*
Baltard: Architect of the Saint-Augustin Church (Paris).
Hugo: *Workers of the Sea* - Verlaine: *Saturnian Poems* - George Sand: *The Last Love* - Dostoievski: *Crime and Punishment* - Swinburne: *Poems* - Goncourt: *Manette Salomon* - *Le Parnasse contemporain* (Banville, Leconte de Lisle, Baudelaire and Mallarmé).

Ambroise Thomas: *Mignon* - Offenbach: *La Vie parisienne* - Smetana: *The Bartered Bride*. Austro-Prussian War (Sadowa).

1867: Retrospective exhibition of Ingres - Courbet et Manet show their works during the World's Fair.
Carrier-Belleuse: *Between Two Loves* - Frémiet: *Pan aux oursons* - Menzel: *An Afternoon at the Tuileries* - Corot: *The Church at Marissel* - Carpeaux: *The Costume Ball at the Tuileries* - Cézanne: *Mary Madeleine*.
Alphand: Promenades in Paris.
Zola: *Thérèse Raquin* - Karl Marx: *Capital* - Mallarmé: *Hérodiade* - Michelet: *The History of France* - Ibsen: *Peer Gynt*.
Death of Baudelaire, Théodore Rousseau, Ingres and Hittorf.
Execution of Emperor Maximilien - Canada becomes an English dominion - French troops occupy Rome.

1868: Foundation of the Société libre des Beaux-Arts (Brussels).
Carpeaux: *La Danse* (statues created for the Paris Opera-House) - Falguière: *Tarcisius, a Christian Martyr* - Manet: *Zola* - Degas: *Mademoiselle Fiocre in the Ballet of the Springs* - Sisley: *Forest Path at La Celle-Saint-Cloud* - Pissarro: *View of Pontoise* - Renoir: *Portrait of Bazille*.
Labrouste: Architect of the National Library Building (Paris) - Completion of the landscaping of the Bois de Vincennes (Paris).
Daudet: *Le Petit Chose* - Baudelaire: *Aesthetic Curiosities* - Dostoievski: *The Idiot*.
Death of Rossini.
Rochefort: *La Lanterne*, a newspaper of the opposition party appears; censorship of the press is reduced.

1869: Pissarro moves to Louveciennes - Monet and Renoir set up residence in Bougival - Eva Gonzalès studies with Manet - Vincent Van Gogh begins working for the Goupil gallery in Brussels and The Hague. Puvis de Chavannes decorates the Museum of Marseilles with his wall murals. Degas: *Jockeys; The Orchestra of the Opera* - Carolus-Duran: *Woman with Glove* - E. Delaunay: *The Plague in Rome* - Manet: *The Balcony* - Monet: *La Grenouillère* (a subject also painted by Renoir).
Alphand: Creation of the Montsouris Park in Paris - Van der Nüll: Architect of the Vienna Opera-House.
Verlaine: *Les Fêtes galantes* - Lautréamont: *The Chants of Maldoror* - Goncourt: *Madame Gervaisais* - Flaubert: *L'Education sentimentale* - Mallarmé: *Igitur* - Sully-Prudhomme: *Solitudes* - Tolstoy: *War and Peace*.
Wagner: *Das Rheingold* - César Frank: *The Beatitudes*.
Council of the Vatican - Rochefort and Gambetta elected - Construction of the Suez Canal completed.
Death of Lamartine, Sainte-Beuve, Berlioz, Huet.

1870: Outbreak of Franco-Prussian War: Puvis de Chavannes, Carolus-Duran, Manet, Meissonier and Tissot serve in the National Guard, Degas enters an artillery unit. Cézanne refuses to serve in the military and moves to l'Estaque - Boudin and Diaz sojourn in Brussels, Pissarro and Monet move to London and discover the paintings of Turner. Henri Regnault's *Salomé* is acclaimed at the Salon.
Frémiet: *Equestrian Statue of Louis of Orléans* (Château de Pierrefonds) - Bartholdi: *Vercingétorix* - Barrias: *The Young Girl of Mégare*.
Fantin-Latour: *The Studio at Batignolles* - Cézanne: *The Black Clock* - Sisley: *The Canal Saint-Martin* - Pissarro: *The Coach at Louveciennes* - Renoir: *The Bath*.
Roebling: Architect of the Brooklyn Bridge (New York). Vaudremer: Architect of Saint-Peter's Church in Montrouge (Paris).
Verlaine: *The Good Song* - Zola begins *Les Rougon-Macquart* - Taine: *On Intelligence*.
Delibes: *Coppélia* - Duparc: *L'Invitation au voyage*. Death of Bazille, Regnault, Dickens, Dumas the elder, Jules de Goncourt, Lautréamont, Mérimée.

Napoléon III consolidates his power - Franco-Prussian War (capitulation at Sedan September 1st; proclamation of the Third Republic on September 4th, siege of Paris) - Rockefeller creates the Standard Oil Company.

1871: Courbet (with Corot and Daumier) participates in the arts council of the Paris Commune.
Monet: *Hyde Park* - Corot: *The Bell Tower of Douai* - Monticelli: *Madame René* - Bresdin: *The Haunted House* - Whistler: *Composition in Grey and Black* (Whistler's Mother) - Rossetti: *Dante's Dream*.
The Tuileries, Palais Royal, Hôtel de la Monnaie, Maison de la Légion d'Honneur and the Paris City Hall are destroyed by fires set by rioters during the battles of the Paris Commune.
Rimbaud: *Le Bateau Ivre*; *The Clairvoyant's Letter* - Nietzsche: *The Birth of Tragedy*.
Saint-Saëns: *Le Rouet d'Omphale* - Verdi: *Aïda* - Wagner: *Siegfried*.
Surrender of Paris (28 January) - The Commune. The week of bloodshed (22-28 May).
William the First crowned Emperor of Germany.

1872: Monet moves to Argenteuil, Pissarro and Cézanne live in Pontoise, Sisley settles in Louveciennes. Toulouse-Lautrec arrives in Paris. Verlaine and Rimbaud travel to Belgium.
Carpeaux: *The Four Parts of the World* - Chapu: *Joan of Arc at Domrémy* - Etex: *Danée* - Fantin-Latour: *Around the Table* - Bonvin: *The Nuns in the Refectory* - Monet: *Impression, Rising Sun* - Cézanne: *Village Lane at Auvers*.
Saulnier: Architect of Menier Chocolate Factory at Noisiel - Bossan: Cathedral of Notre-Dame-de-Fourvière in Lyon.
Daudet: *Tartarin de Tarascon* - Jules Verne: *Around the World in Eighty Days* - François Coppée: *The Humble* - Déroulède: *The Soldier's Songs* - Tourgueniev: *The Waters of Spring*.
Bizet: *L'Arlésienne* - Moussorgski: *Boris Godounov*.
Death of Vaudoyer, Hector Horeau, Théophile Gautier.
Eruption of Vesuvius - Beginnings of the Kulturkampf in Germany.

1873: New *Salon des Refusés* - Manet triumphs at the Salon with *Le Bon Bock*. Cézanne in Auvers; encounter with Père Tanguy - Monet creates a studio on a boat in Argenteuil.
Courbet moves to Switzerland - Pissarro: *White Frost* - Cézanne: *A Modern Olympia* .
Charles Cros: *The Sandalwood Box* - Rimbaud: *A Season in Hell* - Zola: *The Belly of Paris* - Daudet: *Monday Stories* - Corbière: *Yellow Loves* - Richepin: *La Chanson des gueux*.
Lalo: *Spanish Symphony* - Bizet: *Carmen*.
Death of Winterhalter, Ricard, Manzoni.
Thiers resigns - Mac Mahon elected President of France - Triumph of the moral majority in France - Death of Napoleon the Third.

1874: First Impressionist Exhibition organised in Nadar's studio, 35 rue Saint-Georges.
The artists selected for the decoration of the Paris Pantheon include Puvis de Chavannes, Bonnat, Cabanel, Meissonier, Baudry, Delaunay, Gustave Moreau and Millet. Ultimately, few would participate.
Caillebotte, Monet and Renoir in meet in Argenteuil. Berthe Morisot marries Manet's brother Eugène.
Frémiet: *Joan of Arc* - Cézanne: *La Maison du pendu* - Berthe Morisot: *The Cradle* - Renoir: *Sailboats at Argenteuil* - Degas: *At the Races*.
Boileau and Eiffel: Architects of the Bon Marché department store (Paris).
Verlaine: *Wordless Romances* - Flaubert: *The Temptation of Saint Anthony* - Daudet: *Young Froment and Risler the Elder* - Barbey d'Aurevilly: *Diabolical*.
Wagner: *The Ring of the Niebelungen* - Moussorgski: *Pictures at an Exhibition*.
Death of Baltard, Michelet and the Countess of Ségur.
Restoration of the monarchy in Spain. Child labour laws enacted. Death of Guizot.

1875: First sale of Impressionist works at the Hôtel Drouot in Paris (prices did not meet expectations). Victor Chocquet begins collecting Cézanne's paintings.

Jean-Paul Laurens: *The Excommunication of Robert the Pious* - De Nittis: *Place de la Concorde After the Rainstorm* - Cals: *The Lighthouse at Honfleur* - Menzel: *Industrial Landscape* - Monet: *Le Bassin d'Argenteuil* - Sisley: *Snow at Marly-le-Roi* . Completion of the Paris Opera House, designed by Garnier (with paintings and sculptures by Pils, Baudry, Barrias, Delaunay, Leneupveu, Falguière, Dubois, Chapu, Guillaume, Carpeaux and Jouffroy) - Viollet-le-Duc: *Conversations on Architecture.*
Zola: *Abbot Mouret* - Rimbaud: *Illuminations.*
Saint-Saëns: *Danse macabre* - Grieg: *Peer Gynt.*
Death of Labrouste, Barye, Carpeaux, Millet, Corot, Bizet.
The Constitution of the Third Republic of France drafted.

1876: Second Impressionist Exhibition organised by Durand-Ruel. Eighteen painters participate, including Monet, Caillebotte, Degas, Pissarro, Renoir, Sisley and Morisot.
Préault: *Ophelia* - Fantin-Latour: *Les Filles du Rhin* - Gustave Moreau: *Salomé, L'Apparition, Saint Sebastien and the Angels* - Clairin: *Portrait of Sarah Bernhardt* - Renoir: *Le Bal du Moulin de la Galette* - Degas: *The Absinthe Drinker* - Sisley: *The Seine at Marly.*
Abadie: Architect of the Sacred Heart Basilica (Paris).
Mallarmé: *The Afternoon of a Faun* - Renan: *The Prayer on the Acropolis* - Duranty: *The New Painting.*
Lalo: *Le Roi d'Ys* - Brahms: *First Symphony.*
Death of Diaz, George Sand and Fromentin.
Queen Victoria Crowned Empress of India.

1877: Third Impressionist Exhibition, 6 rue Le Peletier, with works by Caillebotte, Cézanne, Degas, Guillaumin, Monet, Morisot, Pissarro, Renoir, Sisley and for the first time, Mary Cassatt. Artists' reunions at the Nouvelle-Athènes Café. Georges Rivière publishes the magazine *L'Impressionnisme.*
Rodin: *The Bronze-Age* - Jules Breton: *La Glaneuse* - Degas: *Fin d'arabesque* - Pissarro: *Red Roofs, Village Corner* - Monet: *The Saint-Lazare Station* - Guillaumin: *Reclining Nude* - Henner: *Self Portrait* - Fantin-Latour: *Woman Reading.*
The Museum of Decorative Arts opens in Paris.
Hugo: *The Legend of the Ages* - Zola: *L'Assommoir* - Daudet: *The Nabab* - Mallarmé: *The Tomb of Edgar Poe* - Flaubert: *Three Stories.*
Liszt: *Funeral March* - Saint-Saëns: *Samson and Delilah.*
Death of Courbet and Thiers.

1878: The Paris World's Fair excludes paintings by Delacroix, Millet and Théodore Rousseau. Durand-Ruel organises sale of works by the Barbizon painters. Sale of the Hoschedé collection at low prices. Zola moves to Médan. Duret publishes *The Impressionist Painters.* Whistler-Ruskin trial in London.
Barrias: *Funerals* - Cabanel: *The Life of Saint Louis* - Carolus-Duran: *The Triumph of Marie de Médicis* (ceiling decoration for the Louvre) - Gervex: *Rolla* - Bastien-Lepage: *Hay Harvest* - Munkaczy: *Milton* - Luc-Olivier Merson: *The Wolf of Gubbio* - Degas: *Prima Ballerina* - Manet: *The Barmaid* - Monet: *The Church of Vétheuil* - Sisley: *Snow at Louveciennes.*
Machine-room designed by de Dion - Davioud: Architect of Trocadero - Gaudi: Designs the Vicens residence in Barcelona.
Nietzsche: *Man and Superman.*
Brahms: *Concerto for Violin.*
Death of Daubigny and Claude Bernard.
Leon XIII named Pope. Humbert the First King of Italy.

1879: Fourth Impressionist Exposition, 28 avenue de l'Opéra. Paintings by Degas, Caillebotte, Cassatt, Monet, Pissarro and sculpture by Gauguin. Renoir exhibits at La Vie Moderne, founded by Charpentier. Rodolphe Salis at the Chat Noir.
Dalou begins *Le Triomphe de la République* - Clésinger: *La Comédie d'Alfred de Musset* - Frémiet: *Saint Michel* - Cézanne: *The Bridge at Maincy* - Carrière: *The Young Mother* - Manet:

At Père Lathuille's - Redon: *In the Dream* - Renoir: *Madame Charpentier and Her Children*. The Facteur Cheval begins constructing The Ideal Palace - Grasset: decoration of the Chat Noir. Creation of Tiffany and Company in New York.

J.K. Huysmans: *The Vatard Sisters* - Loti: *Aziyadé* - Ibsen: *The Doll's House* - Strindberg: *The Red Room* — Ruskin: *The Stones of Venice* - Vallès: *The Infant*.

Rimski-Korsakov: *The Night of May*.

Death of Thomas Couture, Daumier, Préault and Viollet-le-Duc.

Mac Mahon resigns; Jules Grévy elected President of France. Jules Guesde founds the Workers' Party. Jules Ferry appointed minister of education.

1880: Fifth Impressionist Exhibition, 10 rue des Pyramides. Works by Bracquemond, Caillebotte, Cassatt, Degas, Gauguin, Guillaumin, Morisot and Pissarro.

Bartholdi: *The Lion of Belfort* - Rodin works on *The Gates of Hell* - Cormon: *Cain* - Roll: *Striking Miners* - Cézanne: the series of *Bathers*.

Lefuel completes the renovation of the Louvre.

Verlaine: *Sagesse* - Germain Nouveau: *The Doctrine of Love* - Loti: *The Marriage of Loti* - Zola: *Evenings in Médan* - Maupassant: *Boule de Suif* - Huysmans: *Parisian Sketches* - Léon Bloy: *Desperation* - Taine: *The Philosophy of Art* - Flaubert: *Bouvard and Pécuchet* (unfinished).

Eric Satie: *Three Gymnopédies* - Mahler: *Lieder* - Borodine: *On the Steppes of Central Asia* - Offenbach: *Tales of Hoffmann*.

Death of George Eliot, Flaubert and Offenbach.

July 14th declared a national holiday in France. Creation of high schools for girls. Jesuits expelled from France.

1881: Sixth Impressionist Exposition, 35 boulevard des Capucines. The thirteen participating painters include Cassatt, Gauguin, Guillaumin, Morisot and Pissarro.

Barrias: *The Defence of Paris* - Degas: *Grande Danseuse habillée* - Puvis de Chavannes: *Le Pauvre Pêcheur* - Manet: *The Bar of the Folies-Bergère* - Renoir: *The Boaters' Luncheon* - Redon: *The Smiling Spider* - Pissarro: *Peasant Girl Resting*.

Robert de Montesquiou's interior decoration attracts the Parisian art and literary world.

Maupassant: *La Maison Tellier* - Verlaine: *Wisdom* - Anatole France: *The Crime of Sylvestre Bonnard* - Daudet: *Numa Roumestan* - Huysmans: *En ménage* - Henry James: *The Portrait of a Lady*.

Tchaikovsky: *Mazeppa* - Massenet: *Hérodiade* - D'Indy: *Wallenstein*. Death of Moussorgski and Dostoievski.

Antonin Proust appointed Minister of Fine Arts. The Jules Ferry Law passed. The French establish themselves in Tunisia. Assassination of Czar Alexandre II, succession of Alexandre III.

1882: Seventh Impressionist Exhibition organized by Durand-Ruel at 251 rue Saint-Honoré; works by Caillebotte, Gauguin, Guillaumin, Monet, Morisot, Pissarro, Renoir and Sisley.

Courbet Retrospective at the National School of Fine Arts. Sisley moves to Moret; Toulouse-Lautrec frequents the Atelier Cormon.

Jean-Paul Laurens paints *The Last Moments of Saint Geneviève* for the Pantheon of Paris - Cézanne: *L'Estaque* - Lhermitte: *The Harvesters* - Roll: *July 14th Celebration* - Ensor: *Woman Eating Oysters*.

Inauguration of the Hôtel de Ville de Paris (the Paris City Hall), designed by Ballu and Depestres - Wallot: The Reichstag Building (Berlin) - Street: Lax Courts (London) - Bouwen and Boïjen: Architects of the Crédit Lyonnais Building (Paris).

Henry Becque: *The Crows* - Georges Ohnet: *The Master of the Forges*. D'Annunzio: *Canto Nuovo*.

César Franck: *Le Chasseur maudit* - Wagner: *Parsifal* - Fauré: *Requiem*.

Death of Rossetti and Emerson.

In France, school becomes obligatory for children from six to thirteen years old. Bankruptcy of the Union Générale Bank. Death of Gambetta and Garibaldi. Egypt falls under British rule.

1883: Impressionist exhibitions organized in London, Berlin and Rotterdam. The *Salon des Incohérents*. Monet moves to Giverny and Pissarro to Osny.

Frémiet: *The Snake Charmer* - Falguière: *Asia* - Whistler: *Portrait in Grey* - Rochegrosse: *Andromaque* - Cazin: *The Depart of Judith* - Redon: *The Apparition*.

Gaudi begins construction of the Church of the Sacred Family in Barcelona - W. Lebaron, Jenney: Architects of the world's first sky-scraper in Chicago - F. von Schmidt: Rathaus (Vienna).

Zola: *Au bonheur des dames* - Verlaine: *The Damned Poets* - Huysmans: *Modern Art* - Loti: *My Brother Yves* - Villiers de l'Isle-Adam: *Cruel Stories* - Bourget: *Essay on Contemporary Psychology* - Stevenson: *Treasure Island*.

Death of Manet, Gustave Doré, Wagner, Marx and Tourgueniev.

French supremacy in Southeast Asia and Madagascar. Plekhanov creates the Russian Socialist Party. Bismark creates a social security system.

1884: Retrospective exhibition of Manet at the National School of Fine Arts in Paris. First Salon of the Independents. Creation of the "XX Exhibition" in Brussels.

Rodin: *Victor Hugo* - Bourdelle: *Suspended Man* - Marie Bashkirtseff: *The Meeting* - Bastien-Lepage: *The Forge* - Gérôme: *Slave Market in Rome* - Luminais: *The Escape of Gradlon* - Puvis de Chavannes: *The Sacred Wood* - Degas: *Women Ironing* - Seurat: *Bathers at Asnières* - Félicien Rops: *The Temptation of Saint Anthony*

Sacconi: Victor-Emmanuel Monument (Rome) - Eiffel: Construction of a metallic viaduct at Gabarit - Steindl: Design of the House of Parliament in Budapest.

Daudet: *Sappho* - Huysmans: *A rebours* - Péladan: *The Supreme Vice* - Leconte de Lisle: *Tragic Poems* - Bourges: *The Twilight of the Gods* - Montépin: *Girl Carrying Bread* - Ibsen: *The Wild Duck*.

Massenet: *Manon* - Duparc: *A Past Life* - Debussy: *Apparition*. Death of Makart, Smetana and Dagnan-Bouveret.

The Congo becomes a Belgian colony.

1885: Delacroix exhibition organized at the National School of Fine Arts in Paris. Dujardin publishes *La Revue wagnérienne*.

Rodin: *Danaïde* - Carrière: *The Sick Child* - Fantin-Latour: *Around the Piano* - Seurat: *La Grande-Jatte* - Van Gogh: *The Potato Eaters*.

Cuijpers: Rijksmueum Building (Amsterdam).

Zola: *Germinal* - Jules Laforgue: *The Complaints* - Daudet: *Tartarin in the Alps* - Verlaine: *Jadis et naguère* - Maupassant: *Bel-Ami* - Bourget: *Cruel Enigma* - Theuriet: *The House of the Two Beards* - Stevenson: *Doctor Jekyll and Mister Hyde*.

Chabrier: *Gwendoline* - Liszt: *Hungarian Rhapsody*.

Death of Hugo and Vallès.

1886: The Eighth and final Impressionist Exhibition is held on the first floor of the Maison Dorée; works by Marie Bracquemond, Cassatt, Degas, Forain, Gauguin, Guillaumin, Morisot, Pissarro (father and son), Redon, Rouart, Schuffenecker, Seurat, Signac, Tillot, Vignon and Zandomeneghi. *The Symbolist Manifesto* by Jean Moréas is published in *Le Figaro*.

Impressionist exhibition organized by the Durand-Ruel Gallery in New York. Fénéon publishes *The Impressionists in 1886*.

Rodin: *The Kiss* - Bartholdi: *The Statue of Liberty* - Saint-Marceaux: *Dancing Arab Woman* - Dalou: Project for Victor Hugo's tomb - Raffaëlli: *Chez le fondeur* - Rochegrosse: *The Madness of King Nebechenezar* - Degas: *The Tub* - Monet: *Woman with Umbrella* - Renoir: *Portrait of Suzanne Valadon* - Van Gogh: *The Guinguette* - Caillebotte: *Paris Under the Snow*.

Inauguration of the Luxembourg Museum. The Magasin du Louvre Building opens (Paris).

Rimbaud: *Illuminations* - E. Drumont: *France and the Jews* - Zola: *L'Œuvre* - Vallès: *The Insurgent* - Laforgue: *The Imitation of Notre-Dame*.

Verdi: *Othello* - Satie: *Ogives*.

Death of Monticelli, Liszt and Louis II of Bavaria.

1887: Emergence of the Nabis painters. Exhibition of Japanese prints organized by Van Gogh at the Tambourin café. Seurat's *La Grande-Jatte* and several paintings by Pissarro exhibited at the *Exposition des XX* in Belgium. Antoine directs the *Théâtre Libre*.

Camille Claudel: *Young Roman* - Besnard: *Femme nue se chauffant* - Cabanel: *Cleopatra* - Gervex: *Doctor Péan at the Saint-Louis Hospital* - Rochegrosse: *La Curée* - Renoir: *Women Bathing* - Van Gogh: *Restaurant Interior* and *Le Père Tanguy*.

The construction of the Basilica of the Sacred Heart in Montmartre is completed.

Henri Becque: *La Parisienne* - Jules Laforgue: *Legendary Moralities* - Zola: *The Earth* - G. Kahn: *The Nomad Palaces*.

First performance of Wagner's *Lohengrin* in Paris. Debussy: *The Rites of Spring* - Borodine: *Prince Igor*.

Death of Borodine and Laforgue.

1888: Gauguin joins Van Gogh in Arles. Seurat acclaimed at the *Salon des Indépendants*. Victor Hugo's drawings exhibited at the Georges Petit Gallery.

Rodin: *The Bourgeois of Calais* - Detaille: *The Dream* - Gauguin: *The Vision After the Sermon* - Sérusier: *Landscape at the Bois d'Amour* - E. Bernard: *Madeleine at the Bois d'Amour* - Toulouse-Lautrec: *The Circus Fernando*.

Jarry: *Ubu roi* - Strindberg: *Miss Julie*.

Construction begins on the Eiffel Tower. Creation of the Pasteur Institute.

Malher: *First Symphony* - Dvorak: *Quintette for Piano and Strings*.

Death of Labiche.

First Russian Bonds Floated in France; immediate success. Internationalisation of the Suez Canal. William II Emperor of Germany.

1889: Centennial exhibition of French Art. Exhibition of Symbolist art organized at the Café Volpini. Seurat exhibits at the *Salon des XX* in Brussels.

Creation of *La Revue Blanche*.

Meunier: *Le Coup de grisou* - Bouguereau: *Psyché et l'Amour* - Carrière: *Intimité* - E. Friant: *All-Soul's Day* - Rochegrosse: *Le Bal des Ardents* - Harpignies: *Full Moon* - Gauguin: *The Yellow Christ* - Ensor: *Old Woman with Masks*.

Dutert and Contamin: The Gallery of Machines.

Bourget: *The Disciple* - E. Schuré: *Les Grands Initiés* - Bergson: *Les Données immédiates de la conscience* - Maeterlinck: *Serres chaudes* - Tolstoy: *The Kreutzer Sonata* - Claudel: *Tête d'or*.

Tchaikovsky: *La Dame de pique* - Debussy: *Five Poems by Baudelaire*.

Death of J. Dupré, Cabanel, Duboit-Pillet, Barbey d'Aurevilly and Villiers de l'Isle-Adam. Creation of the Second Workers' International.

Photo Credits